Dear God, can you wink?

A Parents' Guide to Prayer

Dear God, can you wink?

A Parents' Guide to Prayer

Gillian Raymond

Illustrated by **Taffy Davies**

Scripture Union
130 City Road, London EC1V 2NJ

© Gillian Raymond 1995
First published 1995

ISBN 0 86201 937 0

British Library Cataloguing-in-Publication Data.
A catalogue record for this book is available from the British
Library.

Phototypeset by Intype, London
Printed and bound in Great Britain by Cox & Wyman Ltd,
Reading.

Contents

Foreword

Corrine Vanderwerff and I have been in the same women's Bible study group for some time now. We have also served together on the administrative council of The English-speaking School of Lubumbashi, Zaire. One day when Walter (my husband) and I were visiting her on school business she said to me, 'I think you should write down some of the things you've shared in the Bible study group.' Well, as she was a professional writer, I thought I would make a few notes and she could hack them into shape – after all, she was the one who had suggested I do it!

Most of my notes were written during the month before the looting of Lubumbashi, the city where we live. At times, it was hard to concentrate on the job in hand because of the high level of tension all around. Cory first saw those ideas as we sat on the steps of the Belgian school, the safe haven to which we and many others had been evacuated by Belgian troops, whilst waiting to be air-lifted out. 'Do some more to it,' she said, 'fill it out and I'll see it later.'

Back in the UK, friend and ex-missionary colleague William Rea made available a spare desk and the computer in his office so that I could get on with the 'filling out' process. Patient man! He turned up the heating until the room was more like the Zaire I had come from than the wintry London that clawed at the windows to come in. He plied me with hot drinks, dry wit and prods to get on and do some work until I'd got it all 'off my chest'. That makes this book his fault, too . . .

Home in Zaire again, Cory refused to deal with the notes I offered her but made me work at them myself – a surprisingly enjoyable and challenging task – giving time each week to go over what I had written with me, eliminating silly bits, making rude comments over any flowery language and encouraging development where she thought it useful. So when Scripture Union agreed to publish the manuscript, I asked Cory to provide the ideas and activity suggestions which follow each chapter. After all, nobody knew better than she did, what I was trying to say. It had been a lot of hard work for her to get me to write the book!

The activity suggestions she has made aim to help you develop your children's experience of prayer. Some activities will be useful for your family; others won't apply. All of them are intended to be adapted as appropriate to the age levels and particular needs of your family.

I hope that between the text, the suggested activities and the illustrations, you will find some of our family's experiences helpful and perhaps even stimulating as you prove daily to yourself how marvellous God really is. I am praying too, as I write this, that together with the children you care for, you will be able to discover as Walter and I continue to do, the importance, the power and the wonder of prayer.

Gillian Raymond
Lubumbashi, 1994

PART ONE
GETTING TO KNOW GOD

1 Prayer – a relationship

Robin was finishing his bedtime prayers. They were somewhat more stilted and a little more holy than usual. A final, loud AMEN marked the definite end of the prayer time as far as he was concerned. He opened his eyes.

'Robin,' I asked, 'do you think Jesus was happy listening to those prayers?'

He knew exactly what I meant, and there was no hesitation about the reply.

'No,' he said, 'but I think *you* were.'

Too young to pray?
What *is* prayer really all about? Is it important for us to teach our children to pray? Can they be too young for the exercise? These questions and others went through my own mind as I considered my reply. Was I demanding too much of a five year old by setting aside a time every night when he is expected to make a formal approach to God? Why did I think it so important? Do I pray that much myself? How did *I* start to pray? Did I just do it, or did I learn? Do I want my children to learn in the same way that I did?

Both my husband Walter and I are convinced that if our two boys are to have a deep, firm, close relationship with God, they must get to know him so well that he

is accepted as a normal and integral part of our family. But we are also aware that this sort of relationship doesn't just somehow happen all by itself!

When Gavin, our older son, was born, we soon discovered that he was not going to be a snuggly, cuddly child; he was independence personified from the outset. As he grew, we found that he was willing to make a big effort over something that caught his attention and interest but that at other times he would happily sit and watch the world go by. We also found out quickly that he enjoyed his food! When Robin, our younger son, was born, it did not take us long to realise that we had produced the proverbial 'chalk and cheese.' Despite a number of outward similarities, the characters of the two boys were startlingly different.

The characteristics that showed in each of them in those early months remain, but the boys go on growing, and we go on adding to our knowledge of them. We know both boys well, and as we grow together as a family, spend time together and share our lives, we get to know each other better, and enjoy each other more.

If we want our children to know God closely, the same sort of thing has to happen. They have got to have time to be with him – early on in life – to make that initial contact, so that they can come to learn about, absorb and understand the basics of his character. They will need to add to their knowledge of him as they grow, but they will then already have the basic understanding and confidence they need to provide the trust and reliance that will colour the rest of their on-going discoveries about the nature and character of God.

Making contact with God

This, however, raises a question. How do they *make* that primary contact with God? One answer, of course, is through prayer.

Prayer is being with God, talking to him, doing things in his presence, growing up under his parenthood and treating him as a Father. Above all, it is the way that our relationship with God finds expression, and so becomes one of the most important ways by which that relationship develops and grows.

Prayer is the way in which I communicate with God; but I am not the one to start the process. The Bible is very clear that nobody can come to God unless God initiates the contact (John 6:44). However, if God has put it into my mind to talk to him or to listen to him, then it is because he has something specific to say and he wants me to benefit from it. And God does not talk to empty space! If he wants to say something to me, he requires my response.

God is knowable to human beings above all in his character of Love. Therefore I can be sure that any contact with him can *only* be for my good and my enjoyment, since God's love is at its source. But I can only get to know that loving character as I converse genuinely with him. We don't (or at least, we shouldn't) talk to God 'because we have to' as Robin was doing in the anecdote I related earlier. We do it because we enjoy and need the contact with our heavenly Father.

Jesus told a story about two men who went to church one day (Luke 18:9–14). One was in a position of lay church leadership, the other had a rather dubious, somewhat sleazy job. The first stood up and prayed a public prayer, thanking God for the blessings he had received, noting that they had turned him into a pillar of the community and an example to those who took on the more suspect jobs in society. The second man felt unable to share his prayer with the rest of the congregation because he had something on his conscience and had sneaked into church to try to make himself right with God. In tears, he got down on his knees and, unaware of the rest of the congregation, quietly but with deep emotion and sincerity, appealed to God to forgive him. Jesus asked this challenging question: Who went out of the church right with God, the saint or the sinner?

'Going through the motions', however correctly, as our son Robin did, or like the church leader in Jesus' story, does *not* constitute praying. That sort of prayer is centred on me, my feelings and my actions, and is really a form of talking to myself. I pray not because I want God to know about me, but because I want to know about him.

Ideas and activities
I. *'The family that prays together stays together.'*

How and how much do you and your family pray together? Read the statements below and then write A (= always), S (= sometimes) or N (= never) in the box which follows.

1 Talking about God and talking to God are normal for us. ☐
2 We attend church together. ☐
3 We pray together . . .
   - in the morning ☐
   - at meals ☐
   - in the evening ☐
4 When we pray together . . .
   - one person prays ☐
   - each family member is encouraged to pray aloud ☐
   - we repeat prayers from memory ☐
   - we use a book of prepared prayers ☐
   - we sing our prayers ☐
   - we talk to God about our everyday lives ☐
5 At bedtime . . .
   - the children say prayers ☐
   - a parent prays with each child individually ☐
6 Each child is encouraged to have a daily private time with God for prayer and Bible reading ☐
7 Each parent has a daily time for prayer and Bible study ☐
8 We read the Bible together every day ☐

II. The fact that you have started reading this book suggests that you are interested in the development of a good relationship between yourself and God, and your children and God. Look over your responses to the statements above, then use the following questions as a guide to help you plan for the future.

1 Are you satisfied with the amount of time you spend dealing directly with God in your family?
2 If so, is the quality of the time you spend with God good enough?
3 If not, are there areas in which you can see the need for improvement?

4 Could you improve or add a specific activity?
   - What activity?
   - Who will be involved?
   - When will you do it?
   - Why have you chosen this particular activity?
   - In what ways can you make it something special
   and helpful for your children?

Don't forget to look back in a few weeks' time to
assess whether the changes you have made seem to be
helping you all come closer to God. If they aren't,
don't be afraid to stop them and try something else.

2 Getting to know God

When I was a teenager, I had a poster up on my wall made up of a series of cartoon pictures of a monk. In the first picture he was a long way off, mouth wide open, calling loudly. In the second, he was larger and less agitated. The final picture showed him in close-up with a smile on his face. The same word accompanied each picture. In the first, it was JESUS! In the second: JESUS, and in the last, JESUS. The caption at the bottom of the poster read, 'The nearer I get to Jesus, the less I have to shout.' It is a good lesson!

Seeing and believing

It is possible to get to know a great deal *about* someone through letters, telephone calls and so on, but it is only by talking to them face to face, sharing reactions to situations with them and spending time together that I really get to know someone and feel that they can come to know me in any depth. I don't want to share anything that is significant to me personally with people I only know superficially; but with real friends I can share my deepest thoughts and feelings.

Children seem to find out *about* God in all sorts of ways. Sometimes they develop rather startling ideas about him and we haven't a clue where they came from! (A child once asked me why God thought teddy bears were good, but not train sets ...) But it is only by talking to him and gaining a sense of his real presence – despite a lack of visual proof – that they can get to know him properly.

Adults sometimes find it difficult to accept the idea of an invisible God. We know that many things in science are not confirmed by simply seeing or observing them; and we know that many things are not at all what they seem; but we still live in an age that relies heavily on visual observation as proof of the existence and nature of an object. This isn't such a problem for children, who haven't yet been fully conditioned by our adult world and its modern rationalism. Imagination is a vital part of a child's life. Rightly guided, this element of the mind develops in children a creativity and an ability to face and deal with external stimuli in a way that can be an enormous asset later in life. A child without imagination is a child handicapped from the outset in his ability to cope with life.

Our older son, Gavin, gave us a good example of this once. He was longing to play with a shiny pot that was boiling on a single gas ring, but he had recently seen me dressing the terrible sores of a child who had spilt hot water down herself.

'Mummy,' he asked, 'if I touch that pot, will all my skin shrivel off like the little girl that comes here?'

He had imagined the situation that might occur if he did something similar, and it made him stop and think before entering a dangerous situation. God gives us the ability to imagine and project because we need it in our everyday lives and if we neglect this side of a child's character we are stilting a vital area of his development. A child who is already used to using his or her imagination will be far readier to accept and try out the *idea* of God than will an adult who has lost or never developed this gift. And as the child discovers that in fact the idea is based in *reality*, so he begins to get to know God.

Learning from example
If a parent believes in God, and if it is clear to the child that the parent knows with quiet certainty that he *is* real, and considers encounters with him to be a normal part of everyday life, then that child will readily accept the same thing for him or herself. Indeed, because of their less cluttered thought processes, children sometimes have a clearer, bigger idea of the nature of God than we adults do!

When Gavin was five or six years old, we were talking to him one day about the greatness of the God who created everything. We were trying to give him an idea of the vastness and all-encompassing nature of God. But we also wanted him to know that because he is so great and so totally capable, God can be right beside each one of us every moment, listening to us and talking to us individually. It is a difficult concept and I was not sure that he had understood anything of what we had been trying to say. However, with a flash of understanding he said, 'Of course you can't see God. If you could see him, he'd have to be so big that the earth wouldn't be large enough for him even to stand on! If he had to be that big, I'd never be able to talk to him; his ears would be too far away!' (giggle, pause for thought) 'But if he hasn't got a body, Mummy, then he can be big and big and BIG inside himself and *still* come and see me and watch what I'm doing. The thing is,' he continued thoughtfully, 'he's too big to have a body, so he does better without one, doesn't he?'

That understanding is a good starting point when you are trying to get to know the invisible God. It sets the perspective from the beginning, and in this case it showed us that Gavin had a far more mature understanding of the greatness of God than we had realised. Perhaps Jesus had in mind this sort of childlike ability to single out what is most important when he said: '. . . unless you become like little children, you will never enter the kingdom of heaven' (Matthew 18:3).

We must remember that our children need our example to follow: they are unlikely to get to know God well unless we know him too. But we parents need to be ready to learn from our children as well. Sometimes they have a surprising amount to teach us.

Ideas and activities
What is God like?
1 Ask younger children to draw a picture for God or write a letter to him. A picture could show something special which the child feels about God. In a letter the child could tell God how they feel about him or ask him something they want to know about him.

2 Ask older children to imagine they are describing God to a friend. Would the friend recognise God from their description?

3 With teenagers, make a cube out of card. Then ask

them to write one of the following on each side of the cube:

- something they like about God
- something that bothers them about God (perhaps this needs to be in the form of a question)
- something they know about God
- something they don't understand about God
- finally, anything at all about God that they would like to write

When they have finished writing on their cubes, ask them to place uppermost the side that most closely represents what first comes into their minds when someone says to them the word 'God'.

3 Starting out

For many years we have lived in Central Africa, in a country where some of the more obvious evils are part of everyday life. Corruption, extortion, bribery, violence, poverty and political instability are things we encounter frequently. New Zealand and England, the countries where Walter and I claim citizenship, often seem blissfully easy-going and peaceful by comparison when we return to them from time to time on visits. Yet underneath it all, as we move between these societies, it becomes ever clearer that there is a limited number of basic wrongs in the world, and that they are common to all cultures. In the Western world you can substitute the problems of drugs, materialism, selfish irresponsibility, immorality, senseless violence, peer pressure, dishonesty and the need to excel; but ultimately it all comes down to the same thing: me first, and I want *my* rights.

Wherever we find ourselves, we see that most of man's problems come from the same root of greed, lying, hypocrisy, selfishness and pride. These underlying attitudes are common to mankind. In order to find a lasting solution, a drastic realignment of our relationship with God is necessary. The resulting change of attitude brings with it a radical change of lifestyle. If you read carefully through the Sermon on the Mount (Matthew 5–7) you will begin to appreciate the fundamental changes Jesus proposed to this world's accepted scale of values.

The root problems *are* common ones, so we can expect that they will show themselves at an early age in our children. Our own boys are no models of perfection. Frequently their behaviour is governed by selfishness, fear or insecurity, resulting in behaviour patterns that are unacceptable to us, their parents. That is why we feel that it is vital that they should come to have a firm knowledge of God and a strong relationship with him, the God who does *not* change with the prevailing fashion and who actually *does* have an authoritative answer to these basic problems.

Maths is boring!

One day when Gavin arrived home from school I asked as usual, 'Hello,' (hugs) 'did you have a good day at school?'

'Yes thanks, Mum. We're doing a play in reading and I'm going to be Finn McCool. But then we had to go and have maths afterwards. Maths is *boring*.'

'Why is it boring? Couldn't you do it?'

'NO I COULD NOT! And it's boring 'cos I got it for homework. Yuk, yuk, YUK!'

'Do you want me to give you a hand? We can look at it later if you like and see why it was you couldn't do it.'

'Yes *please*. I might be able to do it if I could understand it properly. Otherwise I 'spect I'll be up all night with it! I wish I could do it like Jeremy can. He knows all the answers just like that. He's *good* at maths.'

This type of conversation is probably repeated hundreds of times daily in different families, and it came back to me later that evening as I was studying a passage in the Bible concerning my own relationship with God. I knew that Gavin found maths more difficult than his other subjects, and reading more exciting than the rest. I knew he needed help – not simply the answers to his sums, but a little bit more time to be spent with him to give the explanations he had failed to grasp in school. If he could only *understand* the information he had already been given, he would be able to get on and *apply* his understanding to the problem. But feelings were involved as well as facts, and things were getting complicated!

As I thought over our conversation, it struck me forcibly that we don't have to come and tell *God* things – as Gavin had come to tell me – because he doesn't know them and needs to get that information from us. We tell God things because he is our Father and he wants to help us learn and grow up. We tell him things because we like to share them with him, because we know that he understands them better than we do, and because from time to time we are proud of something we've done and we want him to be proud of us too.

Sometimes God tells us things – as I did with Gavin – so that we can start to understand a little better and learn from what goes on in our everyday lives. It is important to learn the basics so that we can apply them tomorrow or later in life.

We tell him things, but in return we have to *listen* to what he says. Gavin had to listen to the explanation (several times!) in order to understand his maths. When he listened, he found that he did understand after all, and could go on and do his sums and get the answers right. It still took some work on his part, but it was no longer an insurmountable problem to him – that time! It is the same with God. If we simply tell him the problem but don't listen hard and apply the answer, the problem today is still going to be a problem tomorrow.

Because they know that God has the answers to things, both of the boys became used at an early age to talking to him. They expect him to listen carefully to what they have to say! Both of them like to talk to God about specific things that have happened to them during the day and sometimes they ask for his serious attention over things that require further thought or sorting out. This is not just something which happens to be common to Gavin and Robin, but it should be the experience of *everyone* who has or who wants to have a Father-child relationship with the God who cares.

When we prayed together that night, Gavin wanted to tell God all about his maths problem.

'God, I don't like maths, and it's boring, really *boring*. I don't really *want* to ask you to help me with it tomorrow at school, 'cos I don't *ever* want to get to like it; but I suppose maths is important really and I shall *have* to ask you to make me like it one day,' (sigh) '. . . only I think I'll do *that* when I'm in a better mood. Amen.'

So why do we pray? Gavin prayed because he felt the need to tell God all about his current problem; but he also wanted to be sure that God knew what he *really* felt, and not just what he thought he ought to feel. He was realistic enough to know that some day it might be necessary to change his attitude – but he was also honest enough to ask God to take note of the fact that he wasn't willing to change at that point in time! We pray because we need to tell God what things look like from our point of view. We pray because we need to tell him that we feel deeply about some things and their effect on us.

Learning to pray

We also pray because we want to get to know God better, and to participate in a growing relationship with him. You never get to know anyone through just one conversation; you have to talk to them often. You have to share your interests with them and experience many things together. You have to want to be with them and to make time together a priority.

A child learns to talk by applying two methods: first listening, then repeating – or talking. He hears his mother saying the same words, over and over again, and eventually he wants to respond by trying to make the same sounds himself. Babies don't start their efforts at genuine conversation by shouting, or making hard, heavy sounds. Their first words are the soft ones associated with a mother's smile and pleasurable contact. Shouting and crying are associated with other needs, but conversation begins in a loving, caring manner. It should be the same when a child learns to pray. He hears others pray, and then wants to repeat those words, which should be associated with something bringing comfort and pleasure and a smile. A child will learn to pray by seeing others pray – and by seeing the way in which they expect a response, talk about and act upon the answers they get.

Ideas and activities

I Help your children to talk to God about their day by discussing with them some of the following questions (but don't use them all!). The aim is to help stimulate their thoughts about what they can tell God. As you talk, suggest items which could be shared with God and remind them that God is interested in what they want to tell him and in how they are feeling.

These particular questions are aimed at the under 10s. For older children, use the ideas but change the language.

1 What fun things did you do?
2 What made you happy?
3 What did you do to make someone else happy?
4 Did anything happen to make you sad?
5 Did anything make any of your friends sad?
6 What was the best thing that happened?
7 What was the worst thing that happened?
8 Do you need help with anything?
9 Does anyone you know need help?
10 Did you do anything that made you feel sorry?
11 Did you do anything that made any of your friends feel bad?
12 What was the most important thing that happened today?
13 How did that most important thing make you feel?
14 Who did you tell about it and why?

II *A telephone conversation.* Using a toy telephone can be an enjoyable way for younger children to learn about prayer, and can help them to talk to God for themselves.

1 Tell your child that praying is a little bit like talking on the telephone. You can talk to God even though you can't see him. God is never too busy to listen; he is always waiting to hear just you. You won't hear his voice answering you out loud, but if you listen very carefully, he will put good thoughts into your mind.

2 Ask your child to talk to God on the telephone. Use the following as a model for the conversation:
   Hello, God.
   This is . . . (child's name)
   Today I . . . (tell about something special that happened)
   Thank you for . . . (correspond thanks to the previous item)
   Please, God . . . (requests for self and others)
   I'll talk to you again . . . (give time of next prayers)
   Goodbye.

III Children are helped in their learning about prayer by seeing and hearing others pray. Think about these questions:

   - Do you ever pray aloud in your child's presence?
   - When you pray, do you make specific requests for your child?
   - Do you review with your child what you have prayed about and discuss with him God's answers to those prayers?

4 Words from God

Prayer, then, requires some initial knowledge of the person to whom we are speaking. We need to have some authoritative source that we can depend on for accurate information, some certain knowledge that can shape our initial ideas. The most important source of information we have about God, available for consultation at any time and comprising a written account of what he has to say about himself, is, of course, the Bible. We have become so used to referring to the Bible as the 'Word of God' that we frequently forget the significance of that title. The Bible is made up of words from God – letters, stories, poems, reports of events, comments and instructions from God addressed to *all* people and to *each* of us individually. We need to remind ourselves of the awesome nature of what God has given us.

Letters from God
God's letter to us, the Bible, is written from his point of view and in such a way that it explains to me what he feels deeply about and wants me to understand. In reading his thoughts on various matters, I come to share confidences with him and to get to know him in a deeper, more intimate manner than I could otherwise. It stops him from being remote, and makes him closer

27

and more real and important in my life.

Walter and I had a slightly unusual courtship. We first met at a missionary guesthouse when I was passing through the Zambian Copperbelt on my way home on furlough. He was passing through Zambia too, on a long journey back to his own mission station in neighbouring Zaire. Although I already knew his parents and several members of his family, this was our first encounter and we had little to say to one another. Some weeks after my return to England I received a letter from him, passing on some information I had wanted that night at the guesthouse which nobody in the house at the time had been able to supply. This turned out to be his chance, and we began a brief correspondence.

At first we simply wrote and waited for the other to reply. Anyone conversant with the vagaries of the mailing system in our part of Africa will appreciate that soon neither of us was willing to wait the two, three or four weeks necessary for an exchange of letters, and after some time we began writing more frequently. We even managed a telephone conversation at Christmas – one of the very, very few that made it through the system. It took nineteen days of trying every day before I got through! Early in the new year, Walter came on a short trip to England. He proposed to me some forty-eight hours after his arrival and we were married a month later. A month after that we returned to his home mission station as a married couple.

Had it not been for the letters we wrote to each other, such a sequence of events would not have been possible. Those letters were the only means we had of getting to know one another, and we both took considerable care in writing them!

During the period of our letter writing, Walter and I discussed a number of things on paper which it would have been impossible for us to talk about face-to-face at that stage in our relationship. Sometimes it is hard to talk about certain subjects. It's easier to write them down, and then have them in front of you to think over. I remember how eagerly I waited for his letters, worrying over what he might reply to something I had written but would probably never have had the courage to say in face-to-face conversation. Sometimes I wanted to know what *he* felt about something, to discover whether our likes and dislikes were compatible and whether there was any indication that he was coming to think of me in the same rather special way that I was beginning to think of him. Each letter showed something different about the way in which *he* thought and acted, but at the same time each was directly concerned with *me* and my relationship with him.

It is the same with our letters from God. Although we get to know him in a personal and immediate way by speaking directly to him, we can also get to know God by reading what he has written to – and specially for – us.

Instructions for today
As we read the Bible regularly and with eagerness, we will find that some of the information it gives is to be made use of right now. It will apply to today and may be a direct response regarding something I have prayed about.

Once when I was still at school, I asked God one morning to show me whether I should do something particular (I have forgotten what) or whether I ought to forget about it. We had family prayers at breakfast and were reading about David getting things ready for the temple that was to be built later. The key verse was 1 Chronicles 22:16b where David said to Solomon, 'So get going – and may God be with you!' I giggled a bit. This seemed to be a fairly direct reply to my prayer!

My brothers went to school long before I did, so I went back upstairs to my room to read my own Bible passage for the day. I was reading Joshua 1 where God called Joshua to lead the Israelites. The heading in the daily notes I was using to help in my study was something like, 'Get up and go!' It also happened to be the day on which we held our Christian Union meetings at school. The visiting speaker read from Isaiah 6:8 where it says (my interpretation): 'And I said, "I'm here Lord – I'll go!"'

Being scared of reading something non-existent into these three comments, I had still not made up my mind whether or not this was God speaking to me by the end of the day. When it came to bedtime, I tried to explain my dilemma to my father. He grinned at me and said, 'Don't you think you'd better do it then?' He understood my hesitation about reading into the situation what might not be there, but in this instance, what I needed to do seemed clear. God can and does sometimes give us on-the-spot answers from the Bible.

Preparation for tomorrow

Sometimes, however, the information God has given in the Bible seems more suitable for chewing over and digesting slowly, like a cow chewing the cud! It is to be stored away for later use, when I am 'hungry' for it. Maybe it tells me about God's attitude to something in particular, his 'likes' and 'dislikes'. Maybe it suggests that my own lifestyle is based on different principles from the ones God seems to be setting out. In that case, I need to think this over and decide whether or not I am willing to change. Maybe it shows me how God answered someone's particular problem in the past – a problem I have never met but will possibly come across in the future. Or maybe it isn't so much about the problem I shall meet, but rather a principle concerning the way God meets problems, that I need to understand.

2 Kings 6:8–23 tells how the entire Syrian army was out to get Elisha. One morning he woke up to find a

great force of armed charioteers surrounding his home town. He got on quietly with his breakfast while his servant rushed around in a panic. Elisha knew his God well and was certain that this attack was something that God would deal with for him. He therefore prayed quietly that God would let his servant see the forces of God which were there to protect them. 'Those who are with us are more than those who are with them,' he reminded him (16). Elisha then went on to deal authoritatively and mercifully with the problem – and he kept his sense of humour too! Do I need to remember that God can deal with my problems in the same way? Have I learnt to trust God sufficiently to enable me, when faced with overwhelming odds, to react like Elisha, with wisdom, authority, mercy and humour?

Sometimes what I read in God's word might be of enormous *interest* but not of obvious *relevance* to my immediate situation. It's rather like listening to world news: I *might* possibly go to the places mentioned one day in the future, but at this moment I am simply *interested* in what is going on there. But God does have something specific to say to me *now*, and he wants me to listen, so that it can be properly stored in my memory, and brought back to mind when I need to apply it later. Before the looting of Lubumbashi in Zaire in 1991 a group of missionaries from the province of Shaba got together for a retreat. During that time God spoke to us about his call and promises to his people. Many, many times in the tense weeks that followed we recalled lessons we had learnt during that retreat, many of which had a sudden and direct application to our situation. We began to see how it was that God had been gently preparing us for the difficulties that were about to come.

Listening to what God has to say to us, talking to him, reading what he has written, watching how he works in other people's lives – all of these factors work together to enable us to get to know God. We need to learn that prayer alone doesn't make us good Christians! But communicating with God and letting him communicate with us will help us to develop a mature relationship that will affect our everyday attitudes and automatically influence our actions and reactions to the events in our daily lives.

So, how can we enable our children to develop this sort of understanding? After all, it isn't always easy to try and help them put into practice something which we ourselves might have learnt only after we grew up!

Learning together

In our family we have continued something that both Walter and I learnt in childhood. After supper we read a Bible passage together as a family and discuss it with the children. We use a series of booklets from Scripture Union to help us in our discussion. The booklets have comments, activities and suggestions designed for family use and we often find that the passage we read applies directly to our situation. We were most encouraged by the way in which God was able to use the different passages we were studying with the children for our benefit during the difficult weeks of crisis in Zaire in 1991.

During one period of three weeks many of our friends and fellow-workers were withdrawn from the country by their sending organisations. Only a few missionaries and expatriates were able to remain. As we wondered about the implications of staying put in Zaire when the indications were that trouble was coming, we prayed together as a family that God would confirm to us that we were where he wanted us to be. At that time one of our regular Sunday Bible readings was centred on the life of the prophet Elijah. We found that God had a lot to say to us through Elijah's experiences.

Elijah appears, quite unexpectedly, in 1 Kings 17. There are no clues given about his background, family history, upbringing, education or training. On the first Sunday we read the account of how he brought a message of doom for a country whose leaders and people had almost totally forsaken God. Now God was coming to judge them. Having delivered his message, Elijah was told by God to go away to a special safe place, where all his basic needs would be provided for. Elijah obeyed God and went to live by a small river which gave him water to drink and God sent food to him morning and evening by ravens. Not quite a normal lifestyle! But for our family there was a clear parallel with the uncertainties of our day-to-day lives. It brought us the assurance that God does provide for us, always, as long as we are in the place where he has put us; but it requires trust and willingness to act on what we know of his character.

Our next Sunday reading continued Elijah's story. When the river finally dried up, God told Elijah to move on to a neighbouring country where he would send a widow to look after him. God did not tell him her name, nor how he was to recognise her. But Elijah knew his God, and went off to the place God had specified. When he arrived, he asked the first poverty-stricken widow he saw to give him a drink and a bite to eat. She had enough food left to make one last meal for herself and her son, and after that, she told him, they were going to starve. Elijah had the temerity to tell her not to worry about such things, but to go ahead and prepare something for him anyway, because his God would provide for them all. Even though it must have seemed like total madness, something about Elijah made the woman agree and she did what she was told. As she shared the last remains of her food with Elijah, God provided – and went on providing for all of them – by replenishing their meagre but adequate supply of oil and flour until the end of the drought.

Maybe God thought we weren't learning fast enough! He seemed to be reinforcing his lesson about our need to trust him and to be willing to act on that trust, even if the situation was difficult. In consequence, we felt that we had to stay in the place where God had put us, in spite of the unrest in our country and even if it would mean facing hardship. God would be able to provide for us in every situation. In addition, he would be able to use our obedience to bless not only us (the widow and her son were fed), but other people as well (Elijah was given just what he needed). The provision was shared; each was able to help the other; and God was overseeing the whole affair. The God who could provide for Elijah the prophet and an apparently insignificant widow and keep them safe in such a dramatic situation could surely do the same for us in our much less public and dangerous daily lives.

Finally, on the third Sunday of that difficult period, we read the story of Elijah's willingness to stand up against evil and to confront the prophets of Baal (1 Kings 18:16–40). He was certain that God would do something in public to prove himself to be Sovereign and the *one* true God. Elijah's refusal to compromise God's standards led to a great intervention from God at exactly the right moment. Whilst the prophets of Baal made frenzied but unsuccessful appeals to their god to send fire to burn up the sacrifice they had prepared for him, Elijah soaked his sacrifice with water. Then he offered a quiet, confident prayer to God. As Elijah was praying, God sent a bolt of lightning right on to the sacrificial altar where it consumed the sacrifice and the wood, sizzled up the water and even burnt the stones. The people who had come to watch the contest found themselves turned into witnesses and shouted out their acknowledgement of the sovereignty and supremacy of God.

Applying the lessons

We needed to hear those lessons from Elijah's story during those difficult weeks! We felt that, like Elijah, we had a sacrifice to offer in public, and had to be willing to put God to the test without requiring a miracle in our smaller and more personal situation. Our peace of mind, our children's safety, their education, our belongings, our home and even our jobs were 'on the line'. Was God asking us to sacrifice any of them to him? If so, would we ever be able to see a response from anyone who would witness that sacrifice?

As we shared the story of Elijah as a family, the children found it hard to wait from week to week for the next episode. Even though they knew the story well, they were excited to see and hear what God was going to do next. As we applied the lessons to our own situation, so they began to ask what God was going to do for *us*, and for *our country*. Would there be miracles for us too? And were we willing to depend on God so much that we didn't *need* miracles to prove again that he cares for and loves his children? That was a hard question at the time. For us there were to be no bolts of lightning! But, looking back on it later, it was exciting to see how God had provided a safe haven for us too, when we needed it, as he had for Elijah – a place where we were fed and cared for by foreign soldiers whom we had never met before. It was exciting to see how he had taught us to share even what little we had left, and how he had multiplied it in blessing both us and other folk around; and how in the end he had allowed us to return to live in our renovated house, providing more than we'd had before. And all this happened in such a public manner that our neighbours, those who lived nearby and the merely curious became witnesses of what God can do. Elijah wasn't the only one whom God could look after!

Perhaps your recent life experiences haven't been

quite so hair-raising! But the principle is still the same. We knew that we needed very clear instructions from God during a time of crisis, so we were on the lookout for what God had to say. We found that, in his word, he had already said what we needed to hear; all we had to do was apply it. When our daily lives are going along smoothly with few problems it can be harder to come regularly to the Bible with such a high level of expectation; but the more we approach Bible-reading in this way as a family matter with a view to finding out exactly what God has to say to *us*, the more clearly we will hear God telling us whatever it is he has to say.

Built to last
Whatever the design of a building, the foundation has to go in first, and to a major degree it will determine the durability of that building. If Gavin and Robin can learn that reading God's words written for them in the Bible is the most basic way of getting to know, trust and obey God, then they are doing what Jesus himself recommended: 'Therefore everyone who hears these words of mine and puts them into practice is like a wise man who built his house on the rock.' (Matthew 7:24)

Ideas and activities
The Bible is primarily about God. Sometimes, however, it's hard to understand what God wants to say to us from a particular passage. How can we help ourselves and our children to hear God speaking through his word? Here are some ideas.

I If possible, before reading a Bible story or passage with your children, read what happened before and after.

II Ask questions about the Bible story/passage to help your children understand it and apply what they read to their own relationship with God.

* Questions of fact: Who? What? Which? When?
  Where? How long?
* Why? and How? questions
* Questions which help children identify with
  characters and events (eg 'if you had been . . .
  what would you have . . ?')
* Questions which relate aspects of the Bible story
  to our individual lives (eg 'Which of them would
  you most like to be like?' 'Have you ever felt afraid
  like that?')
* The most important question: 'What does this story
  tell you about God?'

III Suggest to teenagers that they ask themselves questions like these:

* What is God trying to say through this story?
* Is there an instruction here for me today?
* Does the story say something about my attitudes
  to God? For example, am I willing to do
  something hard I know God wants me to do?
* What is it that God might want me to learn from
  this story?

IV Drama can provide an enjoyable way of helping children to enter into a Bible story and so learn and understand more. Here are two simple ideas:

1 Ask the children to produce a play based on the Bible story.
2 Ask the children to prepare and perform a dramatised reading of the Bible story. For example, if reading the Parable of the Lost Son (Luke 15:11–31) in this way, you would need a narrator, the younger son, the older brother, their father and a servant.

V Keep a notebook for recording any 'hard' questions your children ask about God and the Bible. Ask God to help you find the answers. If you do, write these down alongside the questions.

Suggestions of a variety of Bible reading material to help all ages read and learn from the Bible regularly are given on page 159.

5 Talking to God

I had a most unusual day in 1979 when I was preparing to return to Africa from the UK where I had been on study leave. During the course of the day I talked to a sick girl who was about to have her third illegitimate child, to my parents, to a close friend, to a film director, to a princess of the British royal family and to an African chief!

That evening, when I was discussing the day's events with a friend, I realised that all the conversations had focused at some stage on the same subject. However, in each case I had used completely different words, phrases and images in an effort to make my comments and answers appropriate to the person to whom I was talking.

The most satisfying conversations I have are often those with my parents and close friends, and this was my experience even during such an exciting day. Friends and family had understood what lay behind my comments, because they knew my background. I knew theirs too and knew the ways in which to approach conversation with them without having to think about it beforehand. Most people find that they need family or a close friend to talk to for those same reasons. You can 'share' with them, rather than simply 'talk' to them. I talk to family members about matters I would not dream of discussing with someone I hardly know!

When we talk to God, we talk as family members or as close friends. When we pray, we are having a conversation with him.

A parent-child relationship

In our family, we feel that every child is a special gift from God. The child is actually God's child first and foremost, and he has given us, the parents, nurturing responsibility for his child. So before our boys were born, we began to pray that God would help us to bring them up as his children as well as ours. This means that we need to be a model for our children just as God in the Lord Jesus is the model for us. It also means that our family life should be a living picture of the relationship between God and his children, and we need to work at it to make the picture a compelling one. That is the best way to show our children how important and delightful it is for each of them to become, personally, a member of God's special family.

Children need to learn right from the start that it is as easy and as important to talk to God as it is to come and talk to parents. Talking to God does *not* require special body positions – kneeling, bowing heads, closing eyes and so on. Nor does it require a set pattern of times. It would be hard to tell a child that he could only talk to his parents first thing in the morning and last thing at night and then only if he stood up straight, put his chin up and clasped his hands behind his back!

Gavin and Robin have always talked spontaneously, making sure that we knew what was on their minds at any particular moment. That is part of their growing up, and part of our family relationship. Children need to learn to talk to God in the same way. They need to be encouraged to talk to him when they have something on their minds, something to share, something to ask, something to giggle about, something to wonder at.

Walter and I have let the boys know that we consider God to be our closest friend, and someone we want, and need, to have access to at all times. In order to develop the same kind of relationship, our children need to have the same daily, informal contact with God.

This is a practical way of expressing the parent-child relationship between each Christian and God. At the same time it expresses the different kind of closeness of a deep friendship and it is one of the basic ways of gaining some understanding of God's character.

This relationship between us and God develops from a two-way interchange. There is talking and listening on both sides. As God's children, we are in a relationship where we have the right to ask things of him. Amazingly, we then find that our God, the God of the Universe, imposes on himself the duties of a Father – which in this case are to listen and to respond.

My Father and my King

When I trained as a health visitor in Britain, I had to learn about the normal physical, emotional and mental development of children. As I saw and assessed children in their families, I developed certain ideas concerning the job of a parent. I decided that the main function of a parent must be to care for, protect and love the child so that it can grow and develop into a mature, balanced adult, capable of making reasoned decisions within the constraints of the community and society in which it lives. In order for any parent to fulfil this function, he or she has to be prepared to be deeply involved in the child's life, making consistent contributions in the areas of example, communication and discipline.

Our relationship with our heavenly Father develops in the same way. Example, communication and discipline are all parts of his expression of the relationship between himself and his children. However there are a few differences between our relationship with God and an earthly parent-child relationship! Talking to God requires that we remember who he is, and also who we are. He is the Creator, the Master of everything. He knows everything, but he also cares about everything and so has set the defining lines along which the universe must run in order to function in the best (his) way. We cannot give orders to God; after all, we have less information than he does about any situation. We can ask for explanations, make requests and comments and ask him for his ideas on things. But we need to remember that as well as being his children we are also his subjects.

As we become aware of our own status, so we will develop clearer ideas concerning the things we want to talk about to God. If we are true children, we will look up to him. We will want to do things which please him. We will ask him questions, expect him to provide for us, look to him for protection, run to him for comfort, expect to be scolded when necessary, and, maybe, punished. But we will also feel in awe of our King. We will obey his laws, love and worship him and feel deep loyalty towards him.

Different kinds of conversation
Communication with God is as vital as communication within the family. What kinds of conversation do you have in your house? We have all sorts! Many are the informal 'share and comment' conversations which cover a vast range of topics – from the sublime to the desperate! Expressed excitement, plans for the day, the sharing of information, asking for help, and generally, the talk which keeps everyone aware that they are part of a family – these are the nitty-gritty of everyday communication.

'Please love, would you bring home two loaves of bread when you come back for lunch? And I need to find that letter from Aunty Gwen. It's her birthday soon and I ought to answer it today.'

We also have more formal, structured conversations. They are often of the 'Daddy, I need to talk to you about something' type. They deal with specific questions, often problems, and require concentrated attention on the part of both the questioner and the questioned, usually in a quiet place where both parties can be undisturbed until the matter has been sorted out.

It is not unknown for there to be the more desperate type of conversation in our family too. 'Mummy, *quick* – I'm falling!' Or, 'What am I going to do now, Mum? I've lost my library book and it's library day today' – three minutes before the speaker has to leave for school! These fall into a sort of emergency category of conversation which is often not so much a conversation as a yell or howl!

'Share and comment' prayers

In our house, talking to God tends to follow the same patterns. We have plenty of 'share and comment' conversations. For me, these often happen while I clear up the kitchen or collect the last items of dirty clothes for washing or clear the debris off the floor: 'OK Lord, before we start anything else we need to go and see how Mrs Bloggs is doing. And I've got to call in at the doctor's for that prescription for the boys. What else? Can't think of anything for the moment. Shall we go?'

Then there are the comments prompted by a specific situation: 'Should I offer to go and push that old lady's shopping trolley, Lord, or will she be offended?' 'Look at that mad driver, Lord! Please keep your hand on him and don't let him injure anyone.' 'Lord, there's fog on the motorway today. Please help those who are driving to act sensibly.' For us, because of the poverty in the country where we work, there are also the prayers that go, 'Lord, is that beggar really in need? I don't want to give him something then have him hanging round the car every time I go into town from now on and bringing all his friends with him. But then I don't want to refuse if he really is in need. How am I to know, Lord?'

These are all comments made to God as life goes on. Often they neither expect nor require a specific, instant answer. Sometimes there is no answer to be made. But they are still prayers, that is, communication between people and God. As such they are a valid and important part of our prayer life, and an important means of getting to know God, of building the relationship with him, of tuning one's ears to his voice so that we are ready to hear the moment he *does* have some sort of reply or comment to make.

Formal prayer times

Then there are the more formal prayers. By that I don't mean prayers from a prayer book, although of course these can be enormously helpful. After all, what else are the Psalms? I do, however, mean prayers made during times that we set aside specifically for the purpose of praying. It is important to have such regular, set times. In addition, I find it can be helpful to spend at least part of such a time on your knees or in whatever attitude for you most denotes reverence. Often I like to try simply to fix my thoughts on God and on who he is and so begin a prayer time with worship. We will look at this important part of prayer, which is often difficult in practice, in more detail later.

In our family these formal prayer times are a daily, individual matter. At least, they should be! Sometimes we find that our enthusiasm, or vitality, or will, fail us! We also try to have a family prayer time every day and some special extra times on Sunday. We have found that it is, in fact, easier to establish the family time than it is to maintain the personal one.

We have tried to teach our boys to read a passage of scripture and think about it, then to talk to God about it for themselves afterwards. This way they learn to talk to God on their own, without needing a helping (or interfering!) hand from parents. Gavin began by following a series of daily readings set out in a booklet, with comments and an activity for each day to help fix the key points of the passage in his mind. With Robin we found this method inappropriate and we began by reading or retelling a Bible story and asking him questions about why God did this or why that particular hero or heroine said that, to help fix in his mind the patterns of God's intervention in human situations. Individuals will find their own methods but good Christian bookstores usually have plenty of information available to help parents find what is the best method for their child of combining reading the Bible and talking to God. Some suggestions are given on page 159.

Emergency prayers

As well as the informal and the formal conversations with God, there are the emergencies. These prayers in my experience tend to go something like this: 'HELP!' No further explanations to God are necessary. When we are confident of the God we are talking to, we can be sure that he will answer these prayers at once. We don't necessarily know exactly what it is we need in an emergency situation (except some sort of help!) and we sometimes find that help comes in a way we didn't expect. Looking back, we can usually see *how* God has replied and *what* he has done. In my own experience it sometimes takes a good deal longer to see *why* he chose to answer in that particular way! Let me give an illustration from our own experience.

It was in the early 1990s that Zaire began to undergo a period of political upheaval and civil unrest. As I mentioned in the last chapter, many expatriates living in our city, Lubumbashi, had to leave during late 1991, and we prayed hard and regularly that we would not have to move out. In the end we and the rest of the local missionary community were evacuated from our homes by soldiers who took us to a place of safety. Before we could consider whether or when it would be sensible to leave that place of safety, and whether or not we could think of moving back into our home, our house had been looted, stripped of every item in it and damaged quite extensively. It was then not possible for us to return to our home even if the situation had calmed down enough to permit it. That was not at all the response we had wanted to our prayer asking God to let us stay in Lubumbashi. We could see *how* God had replied and *what* he had done: 'No, you can't stay; I've made your house uninhabitable.' It was harder to understand *why* he had chosen to give us the answer in this particular way.

We left the country in a military convoy together with our other missionary friends, and went to stay for two weeks with Walter's brother in Malawi. This gave us time to think over the situation and try to make some decisions concerning the immediate future. While in Malawi we were able to contact family members in England and New Zealand and it soon became obvious that we could be of use in England. We had had to leave Zaire, we knew that there was a specific and unexpected need in England; and in a rather perverse way, the looting of our home gave us a sense of solidarity in suffering with those we had left behind. It was like an indication that we wanted to share with them, even if our experience was not one of physical suffering. It also gave us the chance, when we returned to Zaire, to share with some terribly deprived people our personal, real and obvious experience of the God who provides. For God gave us many, many gifts in the interval without our needing to ask for material help from anyone except him, and he gave us enough to have plenty 'running over' which we could pass on to many of the friends to whom we had returned.

These events became a lesson in trust for us, and have given us a renewed sense of wonder at the God who is so willing and able to provide 'far more abundantly than all that we ask or think' (Ephesians 3:20, Revised Standard Version). We prayed that they would also be a lesson to our friends and colleagues concerning the deep caring of God for his people. God has still not answered all our 'why me?' questions but he has shown us through it that he did have some sort of reason for allowing things to happen in the particular way they did. God's generous provision enables us to see that he does not work in a haphazard fashion. He was watching over our lives and knew what was going to be necessary long before anything happened. As a result, we were not overwhelmingly discouraged by events and could begin to trust that he had (and still has) some bigger plan 'on the go' that we are not as yet aware of.

During the difficult weeks of rising tension in our country we talked to God a lot. He left us in no doubt that he was listening and giving us daily instructions. As a family we shared our prayers and, every time, we saw God's responses. It encouraged us to see how the boys were able to accept, in Robin's case, or think through, in Gavin's, some of the implications; and how they began to incorporate what they had learnt into their daily and prayer lives.

The day we were evacuated, Robin asked: 'What happened to my "Thomas" book? Did it get looted with everything else? I really wanted that book, Mummy . . . Oh, well, I suppose I *can* manage without it. But God'll just have to send me another one if I find I can't!' In the end, the book became a minor loss. More important became a missing knitted toy, a real favourite, which was supposed to have been in the car with us when we left the house, but must have been dropped somewhere during the scramble. This caused Robin real distress, and I kept thinking about his comment that God would have to provide something else if he found he couldn't cope. But God knew about all these things, and we had only been in England a day or two when kind Christian friends told Robin that they had something for him. It was a toy knitted to the same pattern but in different colours – not the lost toy, which could never be replaced, but a 'relative'! This toy soon bore the same name as the lost one, but in Robin's mind very definitely belonged to the new era and did not have the sad associations of the old. It soon bore the marks of much loving, and became a proof to us that God always knows what he is doing.

Gavin was more concerned about his reactions and whether he would be able to control his frustrations and anger if we were ever able to return to our home in Zaire.

'Mummy,' he asked one day, 'what will I do when we go back and I see the boy from next door riding my very own bicycle?' It had been suggested to us that this was probably where his bike had gone. Gavin was afraid that he would lash out somehow, as the bike was a treasure as far as he was concerned and he knew that he would not be getting another in the near future. We told him that, even if it was true that this lad had it, it was unlikely that he would still have – and use – it in full view of everyone when we returned. Gavin thought a bit and then replied, 'OK, but I'll probably always have that wondering feeling whenever I see him.'

We found it hard to see a seven year old having to work through such big matters. On our return to Lubumbashi we all went together to look at the shell of our house. I was concerned with the lack of doors, switches, sockets and light fittings, and with the holes where things had been wrenched out of walls or torn apart to make them fit through doorways. This was unimportant to the boys, of course. One of them suddenly made a comment about the bike, and I waited for the tears to come. I was wrong. Gavin put his hands in his pockets and said with a sigh of satisfaction, 'But we're back *home* again now – so p'raps it doesn't *really* matter about the bike any more.'

God can teach young, tender lives lessons about right values that some of us who are older find it much more difficult to learn.

Ideas and activities
Talk to your children about the following to help them think about how they talk to God.

I What would you tell God if . . .

* you had just been given a new bicycle?
* you desperately wanted to be in the school play,

but you got a part with only three lines to speak?
* your dad had just lost his job?
* you had won third prize in a big art competition?
* your puppy had just died?
* you had just learnt to tie your shoe laces?
* you had dropped your Bible in a muddy puddle and some pages were ruined?
* you had just baked your first cake and everyone raved about it.

Substitute other ideas as appropriate for your children.

II What happened to you today that you want to discuss with God? Remember, whether we are happy or sad, and no matter how big our problems or grumpy our mood, it's important to be honest with God. We hear him better when we are honest with him.

6 Listening to God

We can't get to know God unless we talk to him often. This means whenever we want to – not just at formal, set times – but whenever we feel the need or even the urge to do so. We do not just make conversation 'at' God, because the word 'conversation' implies that he does his share of the talking too. We need to be alert constantly, listening, so that whenever he has something to say to us, he simply has to catch our attention and go ahead.

'Listening to God' can be a difficult concept to grasp. What do we really mean by it? What are we listening *for*? When God speaks to us, how does he do it? How can we be sure that it is *God* we are listening to and not our own thoughts, or the whims and desires of the moment?

There isn't much point in saying that you are having a conversation with someone if you are doing all the talking and they are doing all the listening. That is not a conversation; it is an outpouring! We all need that from time to time, but equally we all know how difficult it can be to get on with people who never stop talking. A conversation is a two-way process.

If you really want to get to know someone, you not only need to listen to what they have to say for them-selves but you also need to ask questions and wait for answers. Also, if you spend all your time asking someone questions about themselves but never stop to listen to the replies, you won't get to know that person very quickly!

Since many of us find it hard to listen to God or to understand what we are listening for in the first place, we need to remember that listening to God is something we have to teach our children actively. And we can't teach it unless we have first learned it for ourselves! We need to learn three things: to listen *to* God; to listen *for* God; and to have an *expectant attitude*.

Listening *to* God

A good way to start learning how to listen *to* God is to look at some examples from the Bible. In our home we have many times retold the story of the prophet Elijah hiding in his cave up the mountain while God sent all sorts of cataclysmic phenomena howling and crashing around him. Safe at the entrance of a cave, but searching desperately for God through all the whirling chaos and terrifying noise and danger, Elijah found . . . nothing. But when the noise and action had passed and all was still and Elijah stood facing the outside world again, *then* he heard a calm, quiet voice asking him what he thought he was doing (1 Kings 19).

Sometimes when the boys have asked us how they could hear God speaking to them, and what it is he says when he speaks, we have started with this story. They understand Elijah's position. They know how many times we have told them, 'Calm down first, *then* I'll listen to you' or, 'Don't shout! I can hear you far better when you speak quietly and clearly.' They have been told that they can't expect to hear God talking to them if they are so busy whirling round physically or in their thoughts that they can neither hear nor be heard properly. God rarely shouts, we tell them; and even when he does, people don't always understand what he's saying because the noise can be frightening.

We also tell them the story of Samuel in God's house at Shiloh, a youngster doing his daily job, ready to do what Eli the Priest might need (1 Samuel 3). He woke one night to hear Eli calling his name. Eli thought Samuel had been dreaming. 'I didn't call you,' he said to Samuel, 'go back to bed.' The second time the call came, Samuel got up dutifully and went to Eli again, only to receive the same puzzling reply. The third time it happened there was no sulking, no question of 'Eli, are you playing a trick on me?' or even, 'Well, you can just manage by yourself. I'm NOT coming this time!' Instead, Samuel got up, rather bewildered by now, and went to Eli insisting, 'You DID call me.'

Eli was an old man and had been allowing some very wrong things to happen around him; but he was still godly enough to realise that this must be God speaking to Samuel. So he sent him back to bed with the advice, '. . . if he calls you, say, "Speak, Lord, for your servant is listening." '(9)

Eli didn't interfere and try to hear for Samuel, nor did he offer to interpret as if Samuel were too young to understand. In the end Samuel's young ears had to listen to a message for Eli that had been coming to the old man loudly and urgently from other sources for years, but to which he had become deaf.

When God has something to say, it is important. Eli could no longer hear, so God had to give someone else the message to pass on. It was a terrible message of coming doom without any hope in it – the inevitable results of uncorrected wrong. What a stern lesson for the young prophet-to-be! The lesson was that whatever God says, however and whenever, you must pass it on without shirking. Of course, Samuel was in a unique position. Young people today are rarely asked by God to carry such grim messages, but the lesson is clear: a child can hear when God speaks to him. No outside assistance to hear the voice is necessary, although help might be needed in recognising it the very first time. The listener must then be self-disciplined enough to be obedient and do whatever the voice asks. For the child who learns to listen to and obey God in this way, the pattern is set for a life which can be used by God.

Listening *for* God

Samuel listened *to* God. But listening *to* God has to be accompanied by a willingness to listen *for* God. That might sound rather like quibbling, but there really is a difference. Listening *to* God means that we concentrate on what he is saying when we hear him speak. But there just might be the odd occasion when he says something and we fail to hear. That is where listening *for* God comes in. We need to be ready, to have our ears tuned, constantly expecting that God has something that he wants to say to us in any given situation. Then we will be unlikely to miss hearing him when he *does* want to say something.

In neither Samuel's nor Elijah's case does the Bible state outright that the voice from God was an actual, physical voice. We do not read that anyone else heard the voice. It might have been clear in the thoughts or minds of these two, or it might just as easily have been a spoken word. These matters seem to be unimportant in the Bible's recording of the incidents. What is of vital importance is that on both occasions, the voice was recognised: as coming personally to that individual, as requiring concentration and attention, and as needing a response. It doesn't matter that I personally haven't had such dramatic interviews with God as these people did, because the principle is illustrated so clearly in their stories that I can apply it without requiring other signs. The principle is this. God wants to be allowed to intervene in our lives and has many comments to make in individual situations; but we need to be listening for him or we may miss what he has to say.

Let me give an illustration from an incident one morning in London. I had gone with a friend to watch a royal procession. It was due to pass shortly. The crowd was swaying backwards and forwards across the pavement, moving forward every time we heard sounds that might have heralded the royal carriage, relaxing back when it turned out to be yet another false alarm.

Eventually our ears caught the distant clopping of the horses' hooves as they trotted busily along the cobbled road. The excitement rose. The crowd, now it knew that something was happening, swayed forwards towards the cordon of policemen who were good-humouredly ensuring a clear passage for the procession. A man in front of us spoke quietly to his wife: 'We're getting very near the edge of the pavement – be careful you don't go over the edge or you'll turn your ankle.'

His wife didn't hear, she was straining to see what was coming, talking away at the top of her voice, trying to hitch herself higher by clasping his shoulder and standing on tiptoe. It was obvious that she hadn't heard, so he repeated the warning a little louder.

The carriage came into view and the crowd again surged forward, full of excited chatter and waving arms. Suddenly through the jostling and the babble, the man called sharply, 'Look out!' and grabbed for his wife's arm. Too late! Having been propelled forward to the very edge of the curb, she suddenly slipped over it and bumped hard into the back of a restraining policeman. His heel trod heavily on her unprotected toe in its brief sandal. She hollered and hopped about, cradling her hurt foot in one hand, and at the same time trying to peer over the shoulders of the policeman to see into the now passing carriage.

'Why didn't you tell me we were so close to the edge?' she scolded her husband.

'I did!' he replied indignantly, 'Several times, but you

weren't listening.'

'Then you should have shouted louder!' she snapped back. 'You don't sound as though you care too much!'

The man shrugged in resignation and said under his breath but loudly enough for those near him to hear, 'There's none so deaf as those that won't hear!'

How often we seem to be like that wife! The occupation of the moment absorbs all our attention and we become unaware of other things around us, even failing to hear a voice that we should know well. The wife scolded her husband when she was hurt, being totally unaware of the fact that he had not been so absorbed by the circumstances as she was, and was trying to look after her interests even though she didn't realise it. The husband did what he could, but his muttered comment suggested that perhaps he was used to being ignored.

I wonder how often you and I treat God like that? Things in life are so absorbing or so important to us personally that we are unable to hear God speaking to us, because we are making so much noise ourselves.

When God speaks, he uses a means that will normally attract our attention. Like the husband to his wife, speaking seriously but using his normal voice, we can expect that most of the time God will bring things to our attention without bells, thunder or lightening. He will simply cause us to be aware of something that is related to, but outside, the normal pattern of our thoughts or experience, something that makes us wonder why we thought of that at that particular moment. If it is something important, God may repeat himself in a 'louder voice', bringing the same thing to our attention in a more noticeable way. If we persistently fail to recognise God's voice, we too, like the wife in the story, might end up in trouble we could have avoided had we been listening; or we might fail to grasp something he has been trying to teach or to give us. If we do fall, we still find that God's hand is holding us

(Psalm 37:24), but surely it is better to try to be aware of God's presence and to listen for his comments in the first place, so that we can hear and respond appropriately when he has something to say to us.

An expectant attitude
We have a friend who lives in a community where there have been several 'cot-deaths' – unexplained deaths of apparently normal babies aged between about three and eighteen months. Once when we were with her, I could see her head tilted slightly, all senses alert while she talked to me, although it was quite obvious that I was not the cause of the heightened awareness. When I asked what she was waiting for, she replied, 'I'm listening out for Stephanie to make sure she's still OK.' Stephanie was her young baby, asleep in another room.

In our Christian lives, this 'listening out' attitude – which is alert to silences as well as to sounds – is one which *expects* that God will want to say something any moment now. It is the reverse of the *laissez-faire* attitude which tends to leave us surprised when we see God actually doing something that affects us. This expectant attitude is one we ought, as Christians, to be cultivating.

Listening *for* God requires that we see ourselves and God as doing everything together, and that we expect him to make comments as situations arise. Listening for 'promptings' becomes a natural thing once we learn to have the courage of our convictions and act on them – and see that this works. However it only works when we allow it to! Not only do we need to be 'listening out' in the first place, we then need to make an appropriate response.

Learning to listen
To help our boys learn about listening to God, we tell them this: 'When you talk to God, leave spaces where

God can answer. When you want to know something, ask him to lead you to the answer – only don't think that you might know the answer first. He'll tell you in his own way. Keep your eyes, ears and minds open. Don't bombard God with demands and questions without waiting for a response.'

The idea goes in quickly; it's not hard to insert a silence into a prayer. It's like a game. However, putting that silence to its proper use is a practice that comes more slowly. Gavin realised for the first time that God really does speak to us when my friend Jill came out to work in our city on a short-term contract. She arrived, but her suitcases didn't! What the boys did not know was that the missing suitcase also contained presents for their two imminent birthdays. Nonetheless, for several weeks they prayed every night for the safe-keeping of the suitcase and for its speedy arrival. They giggled to see Aunty Jill in Mummy's nightdress or shoes and told God that she really needed to have her own soon. Then one night Gavin announced that he was no longer praying about the suitcase.

'Why not?' we asked, supposing that he was now fed up with the subject.

'Well, I think it's here now,' came the reply.

'And how do you know?' we asked.

'Well,' came the enlightening response, 'I just think that God is saying that I don't need to go on praying for it any longer, so that means it *must* have come, doesn't it?'

He dutifully finished his prayers without further mention of the suitcase.

The following morning we were in the airline office on business when someone asked to see us. He had the suitcase. It was the day before Gavin's birthday, and a week before Robin's. The boys were delighted to see the suitcase retrieved, intact, after several weeks during which they had been praying about it. We reminded

them that God honours prayer, and that Gavin had been right not to pray any longer for the suitcase. And when he opened his birthday presents the next day and we talked again about God's provision, he gave a big grin. 'Wow, that *was* nice of God, wasn't it!' he said.

God *does* speak to us. He *does* participate in our conversations, and this is why it is important to teach the children that they need to leave 'space' in their prayers, time for God to answer back. It also helps to develop the idea of a conversation between them and God, and discourages the use of prayer times as a 'shopping-list' for God. During that listening time we encourage the boys to concentrate on thinking about God; but sometimes we don't quite get the sort of response we might expect. One evening when praying with Robin, I made him stop and wait. After a short while he said, 'Lord Jesus, aren't you talking to me today then? I can't hear anything . . .' Then, turning an impish face to me he said, 'I don't think it matters, though, Mum . . . when I said that to him, he just laughed.'

Ideas and activities
Here are two exercises to use with your children to help them listen for God's voice speaking to them.

I A listening inventory. You will need paper and a pencil for each person and a watch to time two minutes.

1 Sit quietly for two minutes. Then ask everyone to list all the sounds they can remember hearing during that time.
2 Repeat the exercise, but this time ask everyone to concentrate very hard and listen for every sound.

- Could they hear any new sounds?
- Which sounds, that were there all along, didn't they notice before?
- Why didn't they hear those sounds earlier?

3 Repeat the exercise once more. This time ask everyone to choose one of the groups listed below and focus on listening for those particular kinds of sounds. Ask them to write down all the different sounds in that group that they hear in the two minutes.

* Sounds of nature (eg birds, animals, weather)
* Sounds of machines (eg cars, lawn-mowers, washing-machines)
* Sounds of people (eg talking, working, playing)

4 What difference did people notice in the three different ways of listening?

* General listening
* Trying to hear everything at once
* Listening for a special sound

Did you notice that it is much easier to hear a certain kind of sound if you were listening especially for it? That's why it is important to learn to listen for God.

II *A group talking experiment*. Choose a timekeeper. Then for sixty seconds, ask everyone to talk at the same time. Tell everyone to look at the floor, speak in their normal voice and talk about any subject. The important thing is to keep talking, even if the words you are saying don't make sense.

At the end of sixty seconds, answer the following questions:

1 What did the person opposite you talk about?
2 Which person did you hear best?
3 If you asked any questions during the sixty seconds, did you hear anyone answer them? Why? Why not?
4 Did you hear anything anyone else said? Why? Why not?

You can't expect to hear anything properly unless you take time to listen. When you talk to God you need to give him a chance to speak to you.

7 Hearing God

We need a change in attitude, not only to get used to listening for God, but in order to hear – or correctly interpret – what he has to say as well. 'Hearing' is not just the simple registering of a sound. Hearing is a learnt process, involving far more than noting the fact that a sound has been made. It involves listening – that is, keeping alert for particular sounds – and implies that we are ready to make an appropriate response.

God's voice or intuition
There are people who believe that 'hearing God' is in fact simple intuition and nothing to do with the God of the universe. But what is intuition? One definition is that it is a speedy reaction or response built on stored past experience. Let me give you an illustration.

When a friend of mine had her first baby, I was surprised at how quickly she picked up different signals from what seemed to me the baby's monotonous cry.

'How do you know what he's crying *for*?' I remember asking. She gave me a wise reply.

'Mostly I don't,' she confessed, 'but whatever is wrong, he's going to need a cuddle. If I give him one, then both he and I have a chance to calm down a bit, and I've gained some time to decide what really is the matter.'

When I started training as a health visitor I discovered that there really were different sorts of cries that gave specific messages to mothers. When I had my own first child many years later, I found that I had stored up the memory of this encounter.

One day when Gavin was tiny, I was in the kitchen making a cup of tea for a friend when I heard Gavin wake up and give a gurgle. I dashed through into the bedroom in time to snatch a nappy from the pile and catch the smelly stream of half-digested milk that was just starting to spill out of his mouth and onto the cot sheet. The friend followed me in. 'Now how did you know he was going to do *that*?' she asked, mystified. I felt very smug. 'Oh, just intuition,' I said airily. It wasn't until later that I realised how I had been rather dishonest in not confessing that I had seen the other baby years before make the same sound with the same result, and that it had come back very clearly to my mind when Gavin had done exactly the same thing some time ago. It wasn't intuition in the rather exalted, slightly mystical sense that I had tried to imply; it was simply a quick reaction built on those two experiences. I was not going to be caught out again!

We have to learn to listen for God; we have to learn *how* to hear – or to correctly interpret – what he has to say as well. Then we can respond 'intuitively' too!

Getting the message

It is quite possible to hear God speaking without actually realising that what we are hearing is a message from God. We can simply register the facts, fail to take in their significance and fail to act on them. Sometimes the same facts that have been presented to us and which we understand as a message from God are interpreted in a totally different way by someone else. Let me give another illustration.

When children receive gifts, it is usually the *gift* that interests them, not the giver. With adults, sometimes the gift takes on a different significance because it has been given by a particular person or in a particular situation; it is the *giver* who provides the gift with its value. I was once given a copy of a certain book. I already had a copy and did not need two. What should I do? The old one was too battered to give away and the new one came from a special friend, whose gift I did not want to seem to disdain by simply saying thank you and then giving it away. I decided to re-read the book so that I could at least tell my friend that I had read her copy. When I did, I found that it spoke loudly and clearly to a problem I was then wrestling with.

The book had been given to me by my friend to encourage me. Almost certainly she knew that I possessed and had read the book; but, wanting to bring its message tactfully but definitely to my attention, she had bought me a new copy. This in itself was an act of encouragement and love. The gift was a small one; it did not cost much and was nothing apparently special – just a slim, fairly cheap volume; but because I knew the giver well, I also knew that there was a reason for this particular gift being given at this particular time. I read the book and got the message. Had anyone else given me a duplicate of a book I had already read, I would probably have passed it on or 'done a swap' without too much further thought. Sometimes we hear God speaking because we know him well enough to appreciate and want his input into our particular situation.

Sometimes, however, a message is clear but we find ourselves unwilling to accept it. The moral values set out in God's word are no longer the steadfast norm in our society. Similarly family patterns from the past are breaking up and religious observance amongst those who call themselves Christians is in decline. For some people this is a shouted warning from God about the headlong descent of our civilisation into moral and physical chaos following the pattern of other now-defunct civilisations in their last days. Yet for many other people, what seems to Christians to be a decline in standards is simply an increase in tolerance, and they are unwilling to accept that tolerance easily comes to mean total selfishness – 'I am happy for you to do as you please as long as I can do as I please without interference from anyone'. The facts are there; the interpretation differs.

Recognising God's voice

If we have never learnt to hear God speaking, his voice will be something like the street and traffic noises we hear when we are inside our homes: something in the background of our lives of which we are vaguely aware but which has no direct impact at all on what we are doing. Like the noise of the traffic, God's voice can be there, but it makes no difference to our behaviour. It exists, but is inconsequential.

Hearing in the sense in which I want to use that word implies a *recognition of the voice* behind the words. Knowing *who* has said something can give us a clue as to how important it is. Hearing in this way means that the words derive their value from the voice that speaks them. When Dad frowns and says in a stern, forbidding voice, 'Robin, don't do that!' Robin is likely to stop – at once! He recognises the voice and the authority behind it. When Gavin, on the other hand, says to him, 'Aw, Robin, don't . . .' the chances are that Robin will carry on doing it – whatever 'it' might be! The instruction was identical. The response was determined by a recognition of the voice – the authority – behind the instruction.

Following the instructions

This sort of 'full-blooded' hearing implies *action* following the promptings, a willingness to try something even if there is no apparent reason for it. At first there will be times when you are wrong, but practising obedience in good faith leads to an ultimate and increasing ability to discern what is a prompting from God and what is simply an alternative mode of action presenting itself to you.

One afternoon when my husband's parents (also missionaries) were staying with us, they decided to go out and visit a friend. As my father-in-law was turning the car round in our driveway my mother-in-law came back into the house looking for a torch. It was late afternoon and bright sunlight.

'What do you need that for?' I asked, curious.

'I don't need it now,' she replied, 'but it came to my mind that I might need it later. It's such a silly thing to think about all of a sudden that I thought I'd better take notice. It's happened too often before that I've wished I'd listened when I didn't. I might not need it, but I'd rather be wrong than not listen.'

Sure enough, they stayed out far longer than they had expected. Dark falls quickly in the tropics and they were still away from home at nightfall. For some reason the place they had gone to had an electricity black-out and the torch was brought out.

When we heard the story on their return home it was a lesson to me to see that someone who has been walking closely with the Master for many years was open-eared enough to hear such a small instruction. She was aware enough of the Fatherhood of God to accept that he cared about the little details too. It was also a lesson to me to see that she acted on the 'instruction' given and accepted without surprise the fact that she might be going to need that torch when there was no indication that it was likely.

That night, prayer time with the children focused on Noah and the ark and we were able to discuss the fact that, like Grandma, Noah had had a message from God that was really rather silly – to build a boat a long way from the sea and where it never rained! And he had to put up with ridicule for hearing and obeying God when the rest of the people around him were unable or unwilling to hear.

Those who listen *for* God, hear him. Those who listen *to* God find out what to do. They are secure and at peace because they know that God is in charge and giving a certain 'instruction' because he knows what is going on, even if we don't.

On the other hand, those who don't listen for God are unlikely to hear him. They won't hear the instructions given, and even if they could, would probably laugh at them and dismiss them. But the story of Noah shows clearly who lost most and who gained most in the end. Gavin and Robin learnt that night that it pays for Grandmas (and therefore probably Gavins and Robins too) to listen to God just as much as it paid Noah!

Practice makes perfect

In every area of prayer, it is a case of 'practice makes perfect'. The more we pray the more answers we get. The more we listen *for* God and the more we listen *to* God, the more we hear God. The more we are willing to try out the instructions that come, the more we want to try. The more we involve God in our lives, the more we can see God involving us in his plans. And that is exciting.

I have a friend with whom I have talked a lot about prayer. Once she told me that although she had been a Christian for many years, the idea of 'hearing' God in this way was rather new to her. A few days after one of our discussions she needed to go and get a visa renewed. She could do it today, or perhaps tomorrow. For no particular reason it came into her head that the appropriate consulate might possibly be closed on the following day. There was, however, no real reason for thinking this, and there were other pressing things to be done. Why should the consulate be closed? There were no public holidays in the offing – no, the passport could wait. The funny feeling about the consulate persisted, but there was really no more to be done until the morning.

The next morning, the passport was sent round to the consulate for the necessary stamp. The consulate was closed. Had yesterday's thoughts been a 'prompting' from God? I don't know for certain, but I strongly suspect so! For my friend this is a new and exciting area to explore. We can start to hear God's voice as he makes comments about minor matters, ones that don't have earth-shattering effects if we don't register them the first time. We come to recognise his voice slowly, by much practice. I am now waiting to see what my friend will do next time something similar happens!

Ideas and activities
I *A hearing test*. Try this fun exercise with your children to help them think about how well they listen.

Tell them that if they listen carefully to the following questions they should have no trouble in getting the right answers. (Answers below.)

1 You are the youngest child of a family. The oldest child is a girl. The first-born boy is three years younger than his big sister. The second boy was nearly four years old when the youngest child was born. Is the youngest child a boy or a girl?
2 After the first battle between the Children of Israel and the Philistine army, where were the survivors buried?
3 Which book of the Bible has the story of the twins,

Isaac and Esau?
4 According to God's laws in the Old Testament, is a man allowed to marry his widow's sister?
5 The book of Judges in the Bible mentions a man who had 30 sons who rode 30 donkeys and who were in charge of 30 cities. If all but eleven of the donkeys had died, how many donkeys would have been left?

II Jesus says '*I stand at the door and knock; if anyone hears my voice and opens the door, I will come into his house and eat with him, and he with me.*' (Revelation 3:20)
1 Tell your children that people knock at doors in different ways at different times. Ask them to show how they would knock for each of the following:

* You want to go into Grandma's room, but you think she might be sleeping.
* Your neighbours' house is on fire. They are inside.
* At your best friend's house.
* You are the postman with a special delivery letter.
* Your teacher has just sent you to deliver a note to a teacher in the next classroom and you're in a hurry to get back because it's almost your turn to use the computer.

2 Ask your children:

- Did you knock in the same way for each of these?
- How would God knock if he came to visit you?

III Here are two important guidelines to help older children and teenagers to know when God is speaking to them:

1 Ask yourself: does what I think God is saying to me

agree with what he has already said in his word, the Bible?

2 Ask for advice from more experienced Christians.

Answers to *A hearing test*
1 The key word is 'you'. Are you a boy or a girl?
2 Survivors would not be buried.
3 None. Isaac was Esau's father. Jacob was his twin.
4 In order to have a widow, the man would be dead.
5 Eleven.

8 Real conversations

Conversation is two-way communication and a normal part of everyday life. We expect to talk and receive answers and often we don't spend too much time thinking beforehand exactly what it is we want to say. Conversation is natural and covers all sorts of topics at all sorts of times and in many different ways. Conversations with God *can* be like that. Often they are not!

Conversations with God are not the monologue we may sometimes address to him. Nor are they what happens when God chooses to speak to us. They are not 'shopping lists' of things we want to get from him. They are not a set of formal approaches in special language with a special ritual. All of these things can and do belong to the whole subject of prayer, but they are only single aspects that colour parts of the whole, much larger, picture.

So then, what *are* some of the components of a normal, satisfying conversation with God? How can we communicate to our children the ways in which they can have real, back-and-forth conversations with God?

Grunters

I expect you know, just as I do, people with whom it is difficult to have a satisfactory conversation. They are often the 'grunters' of this life, either uninterested in what you have to say, or more interested in what they are doing than in what you need to tell or ask them. When you start a conversation with this sort of person by asking a question, they reply because they 'have to'. To make sure you realise their disapproval they don't make a proper reply, they just grunt. You assume the reply and ask the next question. They grunt again. You phrase the next question so that it requires at least three full words in response! They give just those three words. End of conversation. You have – well, sort of – received the information you wanted from them. They have – well, sort of – participated in the conversation; but it is not the most satisfactory form of contact, and it usually leaves you feeling either frustrated, dissatisfied, uneasy, or all three. Real conversation requires full participation by both sides.

Perhaps we all have the occasional 'grunt conversation' with God! God speaks in many ways, often touching our consciences through the words or actions of someone else. We reply to their spoken words, but our reply to God is found in the attitude or the expression that lies behind the words that made up our reply.

Supposing God has something to say to me about my attitude towards others in need. Perhaps the thought comes, *Help! Mrs Green's been in hospital for a week and I haven't even sent her a card yet, let alone been to see her.* I sort of let him know that I've heard, like the person who replies with a grunt, by sending up a quick, conscience stilling prayer: '*Lord, please bless Mrs Green in hospital and make her well again soon.*'

God is unsatisfied with this response to his attempts at conversation with me so he repeats, or builds on what he has said. The phone rings. It is my best friend. She wants to tell me that she saw Mrs Green in hospital last night and she looks *awful*. The trouble is that she's finding it hard to be with so many other sick folk and she doesn't have many visitors, so she's brooding. I reply righteously that I was just thinking about Mrs Green and had been praying for her. I am hoping to go and visit her (when, I say to myself, I can find someone to babysit the kids on a night when I don't have to help them with homework). My words sound right; my inner attitude is wrong. I am giving God another 'grunt' response. Maybe, just maybe, I will put into practice what I know I ought to do – at a later, more convenient time. This isn't a satisfactory, two-way conversation with God!

In accord with God

The story of the two sons in Matthew 21:28–31 is a useful conscience-pricker about the way we sometimes relate to God. When the father in the story needed his sons' help at work, he asked for it. The elder son refused sulkily. The father went away, somewhat sadly, I imagine. Left alone, the son realised what he had done and, ashamed of himself, got up and went to help.

Meanwhile, the father had gone to the younger son with the same request. This son happily and courteously agreed to help, but then either forgot or found something more important or more to his liking to do. In the end, he did nothing for his father and despite his apparently willing attitude, turned out to be disappointingly unreliable.

Both boys are members of the father's family. Neither is much of an example, but one is just marginally better than the other! When I read this story I am left wondering what sort of feelings the father had about his two sons!

Sometimes we are happily in accord with God's plans and agree that they are wholesome and good; but like the elder son, perhaps through laziness, diffidence or hypocrisy we turn away from the chance to work alongside God, to share things with him and enjoy his company. Companionship is a great and warming extra that comes from amiable, ordinary, well-used, two-way communication with God.

Sometimes we are not at all happy with God and wonder what he is playing at. Engrossed in our own lives (being good neighbours, minding our own business, not cheating, being helpful and trying to be community-minded and tolerant), we suddenly find God asking us to do something that is irritating or disagreeable. Surely that's not what God wants us to do! That's not what ought to happen to us! And we'll do everything in our power to make sure that our rather comfortable lives stay that way. Let God do his own dirty work! After all, he's the one with all the resources. There isn't any real, good reason why I should leave what I am doing now – which is wholesome and worthwhile – to go and do something a bit different.

Maybe the elder son felt that way. Maybe he was doing something quite legitimate (when we reached the place in the story where his father came and called him, Robin's comment was, 'P'raps he was doing his homework, Mum'). But left on his own to think, he realised the basic selfishness of his position – even though he could probably have justified it – and realised too that the work his father was asking him to help with was work that needed him *now*, more urgently than his other occupations did.

Jesus paints only the bare outlines of the picture, leaving it to our imagination to fill in the details; but I wonder what this son did when he got to work. If he was humble enough to mutter, 'Sorry, Father,' I expect the working companionship will soon have been restored between them. If he sneaked along to do his bit on the quiet, I am sure the father will have been pleased, but there might also have been a vague feeling of isolation and disappointment. They *could* have done the job together and possibly enjoyed it. Now, it was done – but barely, father and son each completing just the necessary amount.

Do I ever respond to God in that way?

Regular conversations lead to a deeper understanding between those talking to each other. I am far more likely to do something unusual or something I don't really find inviting for someone I know well and can trust, than I ever am for someone I hardly know at all and have little allegiance to. God needs to 'know' me before he can ask me to do things with him. I need to be part of his family, bearing at least a small portion of his character, so that he can know how I will respond to him, and what he can therefore ask of me.

And *I* need to know *God* in order to understand what it is that he is asking – and in order to be willing to trust that he really needs me when he asks.

In order to set up a useful communication system, you have to ensure that both sides are able to express themselves, and that both sides are able to understand each other, and to be understood. If I haven't developed that sort of communication system with God then I risk missing in my relationship with him that extra dimension of warm companionship that exists between people who are working together on a project for the same goal.

Ideas and activities
Use this activity to help your children think about the *kinds* of conversation they have with God.

1 Read the Parable of the Two Sons (Matthew 21:28–31).

2 Explain to your children that you are going to make up a play based on the story you've just read. Begin with this dialogue:

Mum (*pleasant, smiling*): Ben (Amy)! Come and help me with the washing up please.
Ben/Amy (*annoyed, making a face*): I don't want to! I'm watching television.

3 Pause and ask: How do you think Ben/Amy feels inside about speaking to Mum so rudely? (eg good, bad, happy, sad, guilty, sorry)
4 Now ask the child who is playing the part of Ben/Amy to imagine that they are like the first son in Jesus's story. Continue the play showing what he/she does and says next to him/herself and Mum.
5 Repeat the exercise. Swop parts if more than one child is involved. This time ask the child who is Ben/Amy to imagine that they are like the second son in Jesus's story.
6 Ask your children:

- Who did what was best?
- What even better things could they have said and done?
- What does Jesus' story teach us about our conversations with God?

PART TWO
BUILDING THE
RELATIONSHIP

9 *Teaspoon prayers*

Prayer is usually the way in which we first make personal contact with God. It is also something we have to use to build and develop that relationship. It is a means of learning, of asking questions and receiving answers; a means of passing on information or ideas and clarifying attitudes and thoughts. It is a means of sorting out our frustrations, telling God what we think he needs to know or what we need to tell him. It is an everyday, normal means of two-way communication. The word 'communication' in itself indicates mutual knowledge, understanding and a willingness to put the other person first when the need arises. Prayer is an act of trust in the supreme Ruler who is in control; and it is an act of love and respect for a Father who cares for and loves and builds up his children.

Praying at bedtime
We have used bedtime prayers as a starting point for helping our children to build their relationship with God. Like many mums with their babies, I used to sing and talk to Gavin when he was tiny; and at bedtime we usually ended the getting-ready-for-bed routine with a short prayer as I tucked in his mosquito-net. By the time he was a year old, this had developed into a set prayer which either Walter or I prayed with him every

night. Before he was two, he was saying it for himself. It laid down a sort of pattern at bedtime, committing him to God overnight and asking for help during the day.

We know others who, like us, have made up prayers, choosing words that are applicable to their situation and their particular child. These prayers all have the same general function: they make prayer a normal part of the day's routine; they involve the child in praying; and they make it clear that God is as much part of the family, and as much involved in the 'good-night' process, as everyone else. Our own prayer goes like this:

'God bless Gavin (*or Robin*) and make him good.
Please give him a quiet night's sleep,
And wake him up happy and healthy in the morning,
For Jesus' sake, Amen.'

The children now pray it nightly after all their other prayers, substituting the word 'me' where necessary to make the prayer their own. Sometimes it gets to be mere repetition, but if they don't say it, they feel that they have somehow missed out. As long as they have the desire to pray it, and are willing to do so, it still has a function. Prayers such as this are not only something that keep us all in contact with God, but they become part of a family tradition that expresses closeness, stability and an ongoing relationship with God as well as between parents and children.

When we first started praying aloud with the children, they were too young to make sentences for themselves, so we were in effect doing their praying for them. As they grew, we encouraged them to pray too; and we expected it of them. Some nights one of them might say, 'Why don't you do all the praying tonight? I'll just listen.'

Praying is conversation with God. When Robin wants to ask me something or to say something to me, he comes and speaks to me: 'Mum, can I go and see if there are any raspberries ready for picking? If there are, can I take a bowl out and get enough to make raspberry juice? How many will I need to pick?'

If Gavin comes and asks whether Robin can pick raspberries, I get suspicious. And if Robin stood silently by, just prodding Gavin at the appropriate moments while Gavin delivered Robin's requests for him, I would be most astonished! When Robin wants to know something or to say something to me, he comes to me himself. When we have something to say to God, we need to say it to him ourselves, not find someone else to say it for us. Certainly there *are* occasions when it is easier to get someone else to say something for you; but on the whole it is less complicated, more personal and creates less misunderstandings if you say what you want to say yourself, whether to God or to someone else.

Equally, if Gavin got up in the morning, came silently to breakfast, went silently off to school, came silently home, ate his lunch without a word, went out to play, came in for his bath, his supper, his Bible reading and his story and went off to bed without ever saying a single word to me, I would be most upset and extremely anxious. Actually, being the sort of child he is, he couldn't do it!

We all need to talk to God individually, whether infrequently and briefly or often and at length, depending on our characters, and we need to make sure that we ourselves ask him whatever it is we want to know. We need to say thank you ourselves for the presents – gifts, blessings – that he gives us, and tell him in our own words the things that most concern us.

There have been occasions when we have asked the boys, 'How do you think God feels when he has been with you all day and you haven't even said hello to him? Do you think he really feels like your best friend? If you feel as though you can't cope with prayers tonight, why don't you just say goodnight to him and tell him that you'll talk to him properly tomorrow?'

One night after some such comment, Robin (eyes screwed up and shut tight) said 'OK Mum. Sorry, Lord Jesus. Do you think you could find somebody else to talk to tonight? I think I might be nicer to know in the morning . . .'

Bedtime prayers are a good way to *start* praying with your children, and can be instigated even when they are older. Bedtime is both a family time and a private time and children can be encouraged both to share and/or to have private conversations with God at that time.

Take one heaped teaspoonful . . .
It is sometimes hard to know just how to help a child to pray. What does he *say*? How does he say it? Is there a *proper* way to say prayers?

Prayer is something that develops between an individual and God, and everyone is going to develop their own special way of going about it. The way which works for that individual and the way that makes them feel at home with God and a part of his family as a contributing member, is the proper way for them. Children, however, need some sort of guidelines to get them going, and for us the contents of bedtime prayers have provided those guidelines.

We have established a thank you, sorry, please pattern with our children. This seems to us to be a good pattern for courteous living in everyday life (saying something positive first, setting right anything that might impede the ongoing relationship, then finally making any necessary requests) and is also a very good way to approach God. Acknowledging who God is and what he does for us is a good biblical place to start. It fixes our minds on God and helps us to concentrate. For the boys, it is necessary to remind them who it is they are talking to! Remembering the good things of the day and relating them back to our Father puts us into an appreciative frame of mind and helps to set the tone for the rest of our prayers.

This is also the reason for following the 'thank you' prayers with the 'sorry' prayers. We don't feel that the children can expect to have a good, helpful and joyful relationship with God (let alone ask him to do something for them) while they have things on their minds that they have done wrong during the day and haven't yet acknowledged and apologised for. They need to put wrongs right before expecting God to carry on with the relationship as if nothing was wrong. 'Sorry prayers' are therefore not just a matter of, 'Sorry God that I was a bad boy today' but need to be specific and really meant.

The 'please prayers' in our home come right at the end. These prayers shouldn't be a series of 'I wants'. If they follow from and spring out of thanks and repentance (saying and meaning sorry) 'please prayers' are more likely to be focused on other people rather than on ourselves; and so give the person praying a greater awareness of the wider Christian family and of the world in which God has set us. We like to think of our 'please prayers' as 'responsible requests'.

When I was talking about this pattern to someone, she remarked that this was the pattern she too had employed during her childhood after attending a Christian holiday club one summer. There they called it the 'teaspoon method'. I didn't understand until she pointed out that the common abbreviation of the word 'teaspoon' in cookery books is 'tsp' – which also, of course, can represent the first letters of *t*hank you, *s*orry and *p*lease. She said that their first lesson at the club had been about the way that a small amount of prayer could achieve a great deal, and a teaspoonful was all that was necessary to start out with. Obviously the idea had made a lasting impression!

Having got over my disappointment that I wasn't, after all, the first one to discover that this was a good way to organise prayers, I found that I was glad to know that other people also found this method helpful. That encourages me to go on with it, and to remind the children of the *reasons* for using this pattern when they say, 'Tonight I don't want to say thank you (or sorry) – I think I'll just say my pleases.'

Ideas and activities
Tsp=teaspoon prayers
To help young children begin to pray for themselves:
1 Talk to your child about their day. Help them to decide what they can say thank you to God for, what they need to say sorry for and what they want to ask God for, both for themselves and other people.
2 After talking about things to tell God, ask your child

to repeat the following after you. Explain that you will leave spaces for them to fill in what they want to say to God.

Dear God,
Thank you for . . .
I'm sorry I . . .
Please could you . . .
Amen.

10 Saying thank you

Starting bedtime prayer time by saying thank you seems to us to be the best way to put God in the place he rightfully should have in our lives. He is the giver of everything and we need to remember that and to recall and realise regularly what this really means. Maybe you know the hymn with the chorus:

> All good gifts around us
> Are sent from heaven above;
> Then thank the Lord,
> Oh thank the Lord,
> For all his love.
>
> (*Sing to God*, SU, no. 23)

If we can teach the children the real meaning of these words, then they can start to understand that the root of God's nature is that he is good and that he loves them, individually and specially. Then they can begin to understand that this is why they can come to him to talk to him, whether to express sorrow when they have hurt him or other people, or whether they want to share their excitement about something that he has allowed to happen to or for them. And this is why they can come and ask him things and expect to get a reply.

Once, Robin began his prayer time in great earnestness: 'Dear Lord Jesus, I'm Robin and we went swimming today. Thank you that we could have a drink of Coca Cola when we got out, and did you know the bubbles went up my nose? Amen. Also, thank you that we got a postcard from Grandma today. Please will you tell her that it was the very same picture that our other grandma sent us last week and can she send a different one next time please? Amen again.'

Dependence on God

Saying thank you is, underneath it all, a recognition of the fact that we are totally dependent on God. If we are not careful, this can lead to resentment in our everyday lives. We do not, after all, like to be beholden to an individual for everything we consider worthwhile. But if we think about the things that we are grateful to God *for*, then it puts the dependence back into the realm of the Father-child relationship; and the things we receive from him on a footing of love-gifts.

In our bedtime prayer times in our family, we usually start by going over the events of the day and picking out those that have been exciting or enjoyable. Sometimes there are things that have made a deep impression on the children – what they saw in the street, or the way in which a child acted at school – and they want to talk about it. Sometimes they need to tell us as well as telling God, and sharing their prayers with them can be helpful to us in dealing with their problems. We feel that this is another way in which God shows his love for us as a family, by giving us the means, through him, to be able to help each other.

In Zaire things sometimes happen that we could wish our children were never exposed to, but God allows it. We can't always work through the children's reactions at the time, to help them deal with these situations. Here, prayer times are a great help as the children can tell God what they really feel about what they have seen and heard.

During one particularly traumatic period, Gavin prayed, 'Dear Lord Jesus, I was really scared when I saw the soldiers beating up those people today. Thank you that they wouldn't let us stop and made us go past and didn't want to do anything to us. But why didn't you stop them hurting those people? What had they all done wrong?'

What difference would it make, I wonder, to the children of our inner cities and deprived communities if they could pray like that, with both their earthly parents and a heavenly Father listening to them and ready to help.

Sometimes the boys don't want to say thank you for anything! Then we tend to talk about things that we as parents are happy about, and sometimes we make suggestions about things they might like to say thank you for. They (usually!) take up one of the suggestions and this often then leads on into their own feelings and reactions which they turn into prayers.

Sometimes what they pray does not fit into our adult expectations of a 'thank you prayer' at all, but this is not important. The formation of an attitude that puts God first and stresses dependence on him and the need to communicate a loving response to his care is far more important. The children must be allowed to express whatever they want, since this is their time to talk to God.

'Jesus, can you listen now, please? I need to whisper 'cos Mum's here. Thank you that Léon sanded down the roofing iron today and washed it ready for painting. I loved standing under the dirty water when he stood on the roof and squirted the hose and all the mess waterfalled off the gutter. It was *good* even though Mummy got mad that I was soaked and I got all that rust in my clothes and in my hair. Amen.'

There are occasions when, as parents, we store away some of the things we have heard our children pray about for discussion with them later – at a time when they won't feel that their prayers are in any way being criticised. This is because we want to find out what really lay behind a particular comment. In this way, we can help our children discover not just our reactions, but how God might feel about what they have expressed.

One miserable evening, Gavin was not really 'up to' saying prayers in his usual energetic style. He still wanted to talk to God, however, but curled up on his bed by himself and said his prayers on his own before he would allow us in to give him his last hug and a last 'goodnight'. He started out by going straight to the point. 'Dear Lord Jesus, they say I am supposed to be happy that you made me like I am; but why did you let in the naughty bit? I got into so much trouble today that I wish I was somebody else. Amen.'

Some of the children's 'thank you prayers' are straightforward; some are startling and some indicate areas where we need to talk to them. Usually, they are all sincerely spoken and given to God as an expression of their response to his world.

A good place to start

Saying thank you might only be the start of something: the start of a prayer time, or the starting point for parents to help a child sort out problems, emotions, difficult situations and reactions; but starting out with thanks follows the sound principle that you always begin by recognising the positive before doing anything else.

Saying thank you, we tell the boys, shows that we understand that it is God who is behind all the giving, and that we are actually receiving those gifts. It also shows that we are pleased and grateful for them. In all areas of life we say thank you for things we are pleased to receive, and it makes both the recipient and the giver happy when such pleasure is expressed. It strengthens the relationship between the two parties, and exactly the same thing happens when we remember to pass on our thanks to God.

Ideas and activites

I Ask the children to help you make a list of all the songs they know which say thank you to God.

* Sing some together.
* Change the words of one so that it will say thank

you to God for something special that has happened in your family. Sing that song as a family prayer.

II *A bad day.* When your children have had a 'bad day', encourage them to find at least one thing they can thank God for. Then help them to tell God about their day, and maybe, to ask God some questions about the things which went wrong (eg 'Why did that happen?').

11 Saying sorry

Early on in our career as parents Walter and I discovered that when a child uses the word 'sorry', it is often simply a word to pacify parents and if possible to avert punishments. The word is related to outward circumstances and has very little to do with the emotions, the conscience or behaviour. We soon began suggesting to Gavin that there was not a great deal of point in him saying sorry and then going and doing the same wrong thing all over again.

Say sorry and mean it

In order to explain this to him in a way that he could understand, we told him that the word sorry really means two separate things: 'I wish I hadn't done that' and 'I won't do it again'. We told him not to say sorry unless he meant both.

Some time after this, he did something that had been expressly forbidden and was sent to his room until he was sorry. After a few minutes I went along to see whether there was any progress in the process of repentance and restoration! Unusually, he was in a defiant mood.

'So can you tell me *why* you don't want to say sorry?' I asked. The graphic reply has been with us ever since!

'Well,' he said, thinking hard so that he could express

exactly what he meant. 'I just *can't* say I'm sorry, 'cos I *don't* wish I hadn't done it – and I just *know* I'll go and do it again!'

At that point we had to modify our definition of 'sorry' to become, 'I wish I hadn't done it, and I'll *try* not to do it again.' But at least we were left in no doubt that he had understood the idea, and that he was willing to be honest about his feelings in the matter!

Being honest with themselves and learning to express their feelings are two very important ways in which children come to understand why they react in the way they do. Saying sorry to God helps children begin to learn for themselves that discipline is not simply a set of restrictive rules imposed from the outside. Instead, it is about caring for others – courtesy – based on an understanding of yourself and your relationship to other people. Keeping the rules, whether they are ones that God sets out or ones made by parents to keep family life flowing smoothly, leads to a happier existence for everyone. Learning to be self-disciplined is one of the building-blocks of responsibility, and as we are guided by the Holy Spirit, leads to a real, liberating, deep freedom. Learning to say sorry is part of that process and it is learnt much more easily and effectively in early childhood than later in life.

'I wish *you* hadn't done it!'

On one occasion, when it seemed that the boys had been scrapping for hours, we finally separated them and sent each to a different place with something to do until they had calmed down. As usual we gave them a short time to get over their tumultuous feelings then went to see what was going on. Robin had already forgotten everything, but Gavin was sitting hunched up miserably over a book.

'Please will you go away again?' he asked. 'I'm not feeling very happy.'

'Unhappy with yourself?' I asked, 'Or unhappy with Robin or unhappy with me?'

'None of them specially,' came the expressive reply, 'just unhappy all over.'

I sat down and gave him a cuddle, and we started to talk. He understood quite easily when I suggested to him that being horrid to someone (especially when it seems that they have been horrid to you) might relieve your feelings at the time, but in the long run it makes things worse, not better. Although it might make you feel satisfied that you have 'got your own back', it certainly doesn't make you feel happy.

Struggling to express himself and to sort out the difference between his physical reactions and the emotional hurt he was feeling, Gavin said, 'I just get so mad at Robin when he does things like that. I don't really get mad when he hits me or things like that, 'cos really and truly it doesn't hurt my arms and legs and things. Anyway, I just hit him back and we fight and we usually get laughing in the end. But I get mad when he does things that hurt my *thoughts* – 'cos then it really hurts *inside* me and I get madder and madder and I get so that I want to hurt him worse and worse.'

For him, and I suspect for most of us in fact, it is the frustration that hurts most and is the hardest to deal with, and which leads to the harshest response. In his case, being able to talk it over and express that frustration with a third party (me) who could sympathise with the feeling (even if not with the cause!), helped Gavin to dissipate that feeling and put it into a more realistic perspective. This is one of the functions that we can perform, not only as parents for our children, but within the family of God for each other. It is a part of true friendship and can only be offered or accepted within a close and loving, trusting relationship.

On the other hand we don't always feel badly enough to want to be sorry! Robin, in a similar situation, asked whether he really enjoyed being unhappy, replied, 'No . . . but I want to stay like it till I've finished it all up!'

On another occasion he informed us that he was going to say sorry to Gavin for something. Marching off, he found Gavin and defiantly informed him, 'I'm very sorry Gavin. And that means I wish you hadn't done it, and you mustn't do it again!'

Facing up to guilt

One of the biggest problems in our society today (and perhaps throughout the ages and in every culture) is that we are not willing to accept responsibility for ourselves. There always seems to be an excuse for our bad behaviour or difficult situation, whether it be heredity, environment or other extenuating circumstance. Of course, all sorts of external things have a bearing on our problems, but until we are willing to face up to our own part in any given situation, we will never be able to make a lasting relationship with God or with anyone else.

I once worked on a psychiatric unit where the staff laid great emphasis on the lasting damage that guilt feelings can cause. There were occasions when this was most helpful, but there were other times when I had to withdraw from the treatment team because it seemed to me that there *was* a reason for the guilt. The real need was to help the person face up to the reason for their guilt and, if appropriate, try to make amends. Sometimes it appeared to me that a denial of guilt was being advocated, and an affirmation of self-worth was being imposed which was not based on anything lasting. In such cases I could not accept that a long-term, realistic solution was being offered to the person concerned.

God's way is the *only* sure way. It demands a recognition and a naming of sin, and an acceptance of guilt; and *then* it offers the assurance of forgiveness and of restoration. Only in that way can moral character be built and the need for restitution realistically assessed. This seems to me to be a vital lesson for our children today. If they can learn what sin really is, and how desperately serious its consequences are, as seen in Jesus' sacrificial payment for it, then when they say 'sorry' they will learn to mean it – and will come to want to avoid that same sin in the future.

We teach Gavin and Robin to face up to the wrong they have done, and also to accept any consequences or punishment which result from it. Once this has happened and they have said sorry, the matter is finished, and is not referred to again. This is no guarantee of perfection, but the process has generally seemed to us to bring some understanding of sin, and at least the desire to do right.

There have been several occasions when I have asked Robin if he thinks God has forgiven him after some rather blithe statements at prayer time during 'sorry' prayers. Sometimes he has shrugged his shoulders, and I have asked whether the problem is that he isn't really sorry. If the answer is yes, then we probably won't move on to the 'please prayers' because, I tell him, if you've got your back to God, are hanging your head and mumbling (ie have done wrong but are not yet ready to say so), how can you expect him to hear what you are asking? If you are serious about your requests, you need to turn round and face him (repent); put your head up (show that you're serious and mean what you say); and speak clearly to him face-to-face.

One of the more interesting prayers that we have had on several occasions goes something like this: 'God, I need to be sorry for what I did just now, but I'm not really. If you'll help me to be sorry, then I can say so and go on and say the other things I want to.' And, in our experience, he does.

Ideas and activities
Saying sorry means . . .

* being honest about exactly what it is you have done wrong.
* facing up to the fact that it is your fault – no excuses!

95

I   Ask your children to choose the real 'sorry' in each of the following pairs:

a) I'm sorry I was bad today.
    I'm sorry I trod mud into the carpet because I didn't take my shoes off like you told me to.

b) I'm sorry your car is broken.
    I'm sorry I broke your car when I played with it.

c) I'm sorry I took your chocolates and ate them.
    I'm sorry your chocolates are all gone.

d) I'm sorry the baby woke up and started crying.
    I'm sorry I made too much noise when the baby was sleeping.

e) I'm sorry I broke your pencil.
    I'm sorry your pencil is broken.

II *Sad face/happy face*

1 Give each child two paper plates (or two pieces of white card) and a thick felt-tip pen. Ask them to draw a sad face on one and a happy face on the other.

2 Tell the children that you are going to read some mini-plots. At the end of each you want them to hold up:

*   the sad face if they think God would be disappointed.
*   the happy face if they think God would be pleased.

3 If the children hold up their 'sad faces', ask them what changes are necessary to turn it into a 'happy face' situation.

Here are the mini-plots:

a) Kirsty and Sarah had a bad argument. Kirsty was so upset she stamped in a deep puddle of water.

'I never want to play with Sarah again,' she told her big sister.

That evening when she prayed, she said to God, 'Sorry about getting my shoes wet, 'cos Mum says I shouldn't.'

b) Nick and Tim were playing cars. Tim pushed too hard and broke a wheel off Nick's favourite blue sports car.

'You shouldn't . . .' Nick started to yell. Then he stopped. 'I know you didn't mean to,' he said.

That evening when he prayed, he said to God, 'Sorry that I started to get cross with Tim this afternoon.'

c) Holly and Gary live in the same block of flats. Holly is always criticising Gary's clothes and calling him names. Usually Gary doesn't reply, but one day he had had enough. He grabbed a school library book out of Holly's hands and threw it down the stairs. The cover tore. According to the school rules, Holly would have to pay a fine for the torn book.

That night Holly prayed, 'Please make Gary pay for the book.'

Gary prayed, 'Please make Holly stop teasing me.'

12   Saying please

Probably the most commonly used form of communication in our home is the question-and-answer
one. 'Robin, will you come here please?' 'Mummy,
when will it be time for lunch?' 'Could you bring home
a loaf of bread please?' 'What have you got on the list
of things to do for tomorrow?' Asking is not wrong; it
is a normal part of life. However in my experience,
saying please is much less common. Why is it most
important to say please?

The importance of 'please'
To ask a question without adding the polite 'please'
seems to me to suggest some sort of a duty on the part
of the person being asked. The message is: you will do
what I am asking because I am the one who is asking.
The emphasis is on *me*, the person doing the asking; and
you, the person being asked, are somehow constrained
by my demand. To say 'please' shifts the emphasis onto
the person who has the ability to fulfil the request and
reduces the egocentric nature of the request by allowing
for a refusal. It raises the response options from a sort
of dutiful drudgery ('I suppose so, if I have to . . .'), to
the opportunity to offer service ('No trouble at all. Is
there anything else I can do at the same time?'). For
a Christian I believe this to be highly important. We

sometimes say that for the Christian, life is for service. But it is not meant to be slavery where we do the right thing simply because we are obliged to. It is a life of willingness to put the concerns of others first. This isn't always very easy in practice!

For example, if I were asked whether I would like to work for the Queen of England, I would probably be excited and a little scared that I might not be capable of doing the job to the high standards she might expect or deserve. I might accept, or I might decide that I was not capable of doing the job properly, and so refuse. On the other hand, if I had lived generations ago and been captured in a war, dragged off to slavery and ordered to work in the palace, my feelings about being ordered to do the same sort of job might be very different. If I had thought over the implications and decided that I wanted to do the job, as in the first instance, I would be serving willingly. If on the other hand I was coerced, as in the second instance, I would probably work grudgingly and without feeling that my work was of any value.

God makes it clear that he loves to listen to our requests (although we don't read much in the Bible about his loving our demands) and to fulfil them in much the same way a parent does for a child. With our own children we find that the majority of their requests are simple (for example, 'Please may I have a drink?') and are answered immediately with the provision requested. Some requests need more careful study; maybe they need to be re-arranged a little before they can be dealt with. Sometimes children know exactly what it is they want, and why they want it, but their parents say that they know better because they have more experience or information. We notice in our relationship with God that he is the same with us.

Asking for others

One of the 'pleases' prayed regularly in our house is for those who are ill. We are concerned about their suffering and want God to make it clear to them why illness has been allowed by God to play a part in his good plan for their lives. Occasionally, perhaps, the illness has come though some fault of their own – perhaps an accident because of carelessness or even through deliberate disobedience to God in the past. Then we want God to help the person realize this quickly, set the matter right with him and be able to accept the consequences patiently, to learn from them and get over them as quickly as possible.

The requests the boys bring to God tend to be along the lines of 'Please Father, help Mrs Bloggs to have a good night tonight,' or 'Please let Mrs Bloggs get better soon'. Sometimes, maybe, we remind the children to pray for Mrs Bloggs for the wrong reasons. Perhaps we don't really believe that God is going to heal Mrs Bloggs and we are not even remembering to help the children to be aware of the needs of others. Our real motive is simply to remind *ourselves* to pray for Mrs Bloggs. And when we do pray for her, we need to be ready to move on from the vague, child-like, 'Please bless Mrs Bloggs' kind of prayer. Instead, we need to ask God what it is, specifically, that we should be praying for Mrs Bloggs. Does God really want us to ask for her healing? Or should we rather be praying that she will be able to use her great gift of communication to talk to other sick folk in hospital with her about God's power to help in difficult circumstances? Perhaps God has some other purpose to work out in Mrs Bloggs' life. Are we concerned enough for her to find out what it is and to pray, 'Help her to do what you want,' when she is too physically weak to be able to pray it for herself? And do I really believe that God is using this situation for Mrs Bloggs' – and others' – good?

That does not mean that God does not answer simple 'get well' prayers. The children pray them with great sincerity and we have found that their simple faith does have an effect on the lives and health of those for whom they pray.

One day our boys heard that someone they love very much was suffering from horrible nightmares brought on either by his physical condition or perhaps by the drugs with which he was being treated. The nightmares had been extremely distressing for the family concerned and both our boys prayed hard that the dreams would be taken away. After a couple of days they began to enquire whether his illness was now cured. We told them, no, he was not better yet and could only be expected to make slow progress because his illness was so serious.

'Well,' said Gavin, 'I suppose *that* wasn't what we asked, was it? Didn't we *actually* ask God to stop the dreaming?'

'Yes, we did,' we replied, 'and so far there have been no more bad dreams.'

'I should hope not!' came the indignant reply. 'That's what we asked for, isn't it? But I think it means we'd better go on praying to keep them away, don't you? And can't we pray for him to get better all over as well?'

As 'please' reduces the self-centredness of a request, turning a command or a demand into a request, it also helps us to think seriously about *what* we are asking. Is it really a necessary request, or is it just something I happen to think would be nice? Hopefully, thoughts about *why* we pray these prayers help the children move on from the 'Please God may I have a new bike for Christmas?' sort of prayer towards the 'Please God will you give us some ideas for a Christmas present for Sam? It needs to be something he would really like to have' and, hopefully, this will eventually lead to the 'Please God show us who we can best help this Christmas by sharing what we have with them' sort of prayer.

With both our boys we have sometimes asked them, when they receive something, to give half of it away. We have, for example, sometimes presented them with two treats of approximately equal desirability. We ask them which they want to keep and which give away, and to whom. Children need to learn to share – something that does not come easily to many children. However, they need to see their parents setting an example too, and they need to be encouraged and congratulated when they do share. Guided giving seems to help our children to develop a sense of the needs and desires of other people. It teaches them that they need to bear other people in mind and be concerned for the feelings of others as well as themselves.

Understanding the reply
In difficult situations, God does not always give the reply our children expect to their 'pleases'. But we have found that God himself can teach them how to pray and how to look for his answers.

Recently a friend known to the boys as 'Aunty Eunice' was receiving treatment for cancer. It was causing her much sickness and other unpleasant side effects. She was a widow and we were concerned for her, and suggested to the boys that they might like to pray for her. Robin began to pray regularly that God would make her better, and that she wouldn't need to have this treatment any more. I was reluctant to suggest to him that she really did need this treatment, feeling that this was his prayer and that the Holy Spirit knew better than I did how to interpret it correctly! Two months later, when we had contact with Aunty Eunice, we asked about the progress of her treatment. She told us that her doctor had stopped the particular treatment Robin had prayed about because of the severity of the side-effects, and she had been put on a new, trial form of medication which seemed to be working well. We told the boys. Robin prayed that night, 'Dear Lord Jesus, thank you for listening when we asked you to stop that treatment that Aunty Eunice was having. I thought you were going to make her better, but if the new medicine can do it instead, then that's all right.' He was excited to think that God had listened to *him*, and had given him an answer; and he was quite willing to accept that it *was* an answer, even if it wasn't the one he had expected.

One result of this incident was to spur both boys on to continue praying for other sick folk for whom they had as yet seen no answers to their prayers. We trust that this will be a very positive step in teaching them the need to 'pray and not give up' (Luke 18:1).

'Please' can help us all to become more caring, more sharing and more willing to talk to and depend on the Father who delights to give to his children so 'much more' (Matthew 7:11) than a human parent either will or can.

Ideas and activities
Help your children to think about the 'please prayers' they say to God by talking about 'Amanda's prayer' below.

Amanda's prayer
Dear God, my birthday is next week. I want to have a party with a big cake, ice cream, party hats, and lots of games and prizes. I want to invite ten friends. But Mum says I can't. She says parties take too much work and cost too much money. I don't think so. Please make her change her mind.
Amen.

1 Ask your children:

* If you were God, what might you think about Amanda's prayer? Why?
* What good things might God see in her prayer?

2 Now help Amanda say a teaspoon prayer (see page 82).
Using the information given, help her to:

- say thank you for at least two things.
- say sorry to God for one thing.
- say a 'please prayer' about her birthday that God will be happy with.

13 Just for starters

'What's for dinner, Mum? . . . Yum! my favourite! I'm hungry!'

'Go and put your school bag down and wash your hands, then we can start.'

Two minutes later:

'I'm not going to say thank you before I have my lunch today.'

'Aren't you? Any reason?'

'Because I'm just going to eat it, that's all. Why do I have to say 'please' and 'thank you' all the time?'

'You don't, but when I give you something you've been wanting, you usually feel happy and come and give me a hug, then I'm pleased. God's given us what we need to make lunch, and it's a nice one; don't you want to let him know that you're pleased with it?'

Saying grace

'Grace' before meals is a short prayer of thanks for the food that has been provided and an acknowledgement that, whoever paid for it and whoever prepared it, ultimately the meal has been given by God. Saying 'grace' is one good way of getting a child used to praying. Recognising God's gifts and saying thank you is important. In much the same way that we teach children good manners in other areas of their lives we need to teach them good manners towards God too.

Sometimes we pray a formal prayer; sometimes say an appropriate rhyme; sometimes one person prays for all of us; sometimes we sing something suitable together. The only really consistent things are that we say grace before every meal, and that we hold hands while we do it. I suppose holding hands is one good way of being sure that little hands don't have sneaky pickings while other eyes are closed! But that's not the real reason for holding hands. In the midst of a busy life, we share our meal *together*. It is an enjoyable time when we can share thoughts and feelings as a family. The meal has been given to us by God as a *family*, and so we all want to send him our thanks together, as a single unit. Holding hands demonstrates this.

Giving thanks for a meal is not of itself a major part of our development as Christians, and it can easily become just another habit. However it is a good habit, and can still have a part to play in our lives even when we have temporarily forgotten why we do it. We don't let our own children stop saying 'please' and 'thank you' just because most of the time they are not thinking about what they are saying when they use those words. They are part of a code of courtesy that has an effect on the lives of others, creating small feelings of warmth, opening up possibilities for kindness and service which remain closed in the less caring, colder and more stark atmosphere where they are not used. We love God and, particularly in our case where we are living in a poor country, we want our boys to realize that God has blessed them in many ways and with many things. They must be prepared to think about that from time to time and remember that it is because God loves people that he gives. And because they love him, their natural response should be to want to say thank you.

Praying alone

'I think I'll pray by myself tonight, Mum,' came the comment as I pulled down the mosquito-net and prepared to sit on Gavin's bed for the usual bedtime prayers.

'OK,' I replied. 'Any special reason, or is it just that you feel like it?'

'Well,' came the somewhat reluctant reply, 'I've got rather a lot of sorry prayers to say tonight and I think I'd rather be private.'

Praying is contact between the individual and God. At rock bottom it involves nobody else. Prayers prayed out loud in a group situation often can't be fully shared because individuals feel restrained in various ways by the group. So when the boys want to pray by themselves – and we are sure that it is not just because they want to skip prayers for tonight because of a bad conscience, laziness or simple contrariness – we always let them. There is no need for us to be there to share their prayers if they feel no need of help, or if they simply need to talk things out alone with God. In fact it is something to be encouraged. My own parents were ready to pray with us until we were in our early teens, but between the ages of about eight and eleven years, I prayed my bedtime prayers mostly by myself, because that was what I wanted.

There are several different sorts of praying. In my own personal experience they lead on from one another and all have a great deal to do with maturing relationships either within the family, with God, or with others in the outside world.

When someone learns to pray as an adult, they usually start alone. Until someone wants to know God for themselves, they do not pray. But God has built into man the need to be in contact with him and eventually this need will be acknowledged. Personal contact with God is made between two individuals – God and me.

When we teach *young children* to pray, they usually accept the idea of God easily, but have not yet developed the means to express their thoughts. Parents can help by offering set prayers, or by praying with and for the children. But it should not be long before the children are able and wanting to formulate their own conversations with him much as they do with their parents. Great sensitivity is needed so that we don't simply impose on the children the form of praying we use ourselves. The more conversational our own prayers tend to be with God, the more natural will be our praying aloud with our children. This should allow them to develop their own style of conversation in prayer with God without feeling the need to follow their parents' style and words. As they see us using all sorts of different styles of prayer according to the subjects of those prayers, so they will learn to decide for themselves what is appropriate for them.

Praying with others
Praying alone often develops into praying together. When I was younger, I was much more willing to pray together with my family than I ever was in a gathering of other Christians. Perhaps you feel as I did. We know our family members well and they know us. They will treat our stumblings and mumblings in the right spirit (usually!), and we are neither self-conscious enough to exclude ourselves from prayer times nor self-centred enough to want to monopolise them. Praying together as a family teaches us to share our problems and our joys, and gives others a chance to develop their own relationship with us and with God as they become part of our praying and we become part of theirs. Praying together teaches us to give as well as receive. I've noticed that it is harder for people who have never prayed at home to start praying aloud in a Christian group elsewhere. It demands trust and confidence, sympathy

and sensitivity in the group and that requires a close and loving relationship. 1 John 1:7 reminds us that '... if we walk in the light as he is in the light' (a right vertical relationship) 'then we have fellowship with one another' (a right vertical and horizontal relationship; fellowship with our Christian family as well as fellowship with our Father in heaven). I remember the time a gentleman with a saggy chin, a ponderous voice and twinkly eyes told me the well-known catch-phrase: 'The family that prays together, stays together.' Although a cliché, it remains largely true and is worth remembering.

I found that only after I had learnt to pray alone, and with my family, and in a group, was I ready to pray in a twosome with someone outside my family. It required a commitment both to that person and to the belief that prayer was vital – and that it worked. It was one of the most difficult things I have ever done. It required an opening up to someone else that left me feeling vulnerable and exposed. But when reciprocated, it allowed the development of a power in prayer that was able to be directed outwards much faster than I would have thought possible. I prayed with two different girls in this way when I was at university, and it was an enormously helpful experience.

There are some families where it is obvious that the husband and wife pray together. That is another way of 'praying in twos' and the Bible seems to commend this too (1 Peter 3:7b), although it is hard to start where there has been no previous habit of sharing in this way.

'Dear Lord Jesus . . .'
Our boys used to start most of their prayers, 'Dear Lord Jesus . . .' which probably means that we started many prayers with them that way. This is not wrong, but it raises certain questions about our concept of God. When we pray, who are we praying to? Well, God of

course. But then we know God in three distinct persons. We know him as the Father, who is also the Almighty; we know him as the Son, the Lord Jesus, the Master; and we know him as the Holy Spirit, the Comforter, the Helper and the Interpreter. It does not matter which member of the Trinity we address in our prayers, since they are in fact all one, but it can help to differentiate between them. If we do, it will help our children to learn and understand more about the God they are talking to.

On the whole the majority of requests within our family circle are made by the children and are directed to us as parents. The children know (or think they know!) that we have the means of supplying the need or answering the request. If we are really living as God's children, then the majority of our requests will be made to him in his capacity as our Father.

Sometimes we find it hard to express ourselves. Many times when our children were very young, an 'interpreter' was required so that a listener could make sense of the conversation. Perhaps Gavin would say a sentence or word that was apparently unrelated to anything else that was happening or being said, but we understood if we knew what had been going on in the moments or hours beforehand: a story he had heard, a television programme he had watched, what he'd been doing at kindergarten. His comment or question would be meaningless without knowing this background. Sometimes one parent was able to make the connection, but the other was not – because they were not involved in the beginning of the thought process. Then one of us would have to explain to the other what Gavin had meant.

It is, of course, not an exact parallel, but in a similar way the Holy Spirit interprets our prayers to the Father. Sometimes we don't express the real needs of our lives, or our desires for others very clearly. In some mystical way the Holy Spirit takes our faltering, confused words and thoughts and presents the real prayers of our hearts to God our Father. Because of his intervention (or interpretation) we know that there is no misunderstanding. This is prayer in the power of the Holy Spirit.

Then, since our personal knowledge of God is through the demonstration of his character in the life of the Lord Jesus, and since it is the Lord Jesus we are following, we tend to ask our prayers 'in Jesus' name' or 'for his sake'. That is to say, because we know him so well, we know that something we want is something that he wants, too. We can then have confidence that what we are doing and asking will please our Father, and so he will be delighted to give us what we have requested. When we conclude our prayers 'in Jesus' name', we are in effect saying to God, 'And the Lord Jesus is in complete agreement, so please will you do it?' Such a thought should challenge us and maybe change what we ask and how we ask it!

As we grow more mature in our faith, it is good to think about the direction of our prayers: whom we address, how he knows exactly what we mean, and why he, the God of the Universe, is willing to act on something such insignificant individuals have to ask.

As a starting point, children begin to develop their relationship with God by praying, 'Dear Lord Jesus . . .' But as they grow, learning that the God they speak to is in fact not just 'Son' but also 'Father' and 'Holy Spirit' is important. Little by little we will see a growth in their understanding of and confidence in the God to whom they are speaking.

Ideas and activities
Saying 'grace' at mealtimes is a way of remembering that God is with you as a family, and of making prayer a regular, normal part of your life together. Here are some ideas for 'grace'.

1 Sing a short song of thanks. This could be done whilst holding hands and either standing around or sitting at the table.

2 One person (child or adult) prays on behalf of the family. Take turns so that everyone prays for at least one meal during the week.

3 Repeat together a prayer rhyme. For example:

> Bless, O Lord, this food we take,
> And make us good for Jesus' sake.
> Amen.

4 Ask the children to make up your own family prayer rhyme that you can say together.

5 Round-the-table prayers. One person starts and then when everyone has had a turn, say 'Amen' together.

6 After-the-meal thanks. One person says a brief 'thank-you prayer' on behalf of the family, ending with the words: '. . . in the name of Jesus who taught us to pray . . .' Then everyone says the Lord's Prayer together.

PART THREE
GROWING UP

14 *The God we worship*

'Mummy, can God wink?'

'I don't know, Robin, I've never asked him.'

'Well I think we'd better, 'cos I'm practising, and I'd like him to show me how to do it properly . . .'

Getting to know God

When a child grows up knowing that he can talk to God about anything at all, knowing that he doesn't just have to pray 'at' God, and discovering that God is interested in whatever he wants to tell him, including all his worries (1 Peter 5:7), then that child is developing a sound relationship with the God who wants to be his Father.

Clearly, we cannot get to know God unless we believe that he exists. Even if we believe that he exists, we still cannot get to know him in a personal way unless we are willing to talk to him and listen to him. If we teach our children to find out for themselves what he thinks about certain things, their own attitudes will be shaped and moulded by their discoveries. God's standards will become incorporated into their characters. Parents too need to be constantly in two-way contact with God. This helps us to realise more and more how much we rely on him and how much we need his knowledge of life to help and guide us. Getting to know him better

also changes many of my preconceived ideas about God. Helping our children learn how to get to know God will give them the chance to find out for themselves what he is like – and that might not be exactly what I as a parent had led them to believe!

Encouraging the children to pray by praying with them, and helping them to get on and do it for themselves (not just at night, at mealtimes or in a crisis, but whenever they need to talk to someone about something) is a most important and significant way in which parents can help their children to develop. Prayer plays a vital part in teaching children to grow up into mature men or women of God, alert to the world around them with its needs and joys, and aware of the goodness of God that surrounds them even when the going gets rough. It gives every child a sense of his or her own worth that is *rightly* based, not on a selfish, self-centred examination of personal character and traits, but on a relationship of love with a caring Father whom the child wants to please.

Our relationship with God is complex. Each of us is his child, follower, friend, subject, pupil and object of intense love, but governing it all is the confidence that, if we know God as Father and if we are acting as children, then we are totally secure in that relationship which he promises is only and always working for our good. It is worth repeating the words Peter used to encourage the Christians of the first century. He wrote to them, 'Let him have all your worries and cares, for he is *always* thinking about you and watching *everything* that concerns you.' (The Living Bible, my italics). As we think about *him*, we get our attitudes to *ourselves* back in a right perspective.

What is worship?

What do *you* mean when you use the word 'worship'? In my family, it is a very uncommon word in our everyday conversations. It is a ceremonial or religious word associated with vague feelings of paying homage or going down on bended knee – things we associate with the past, or with ceremonies of state and monarchies. In England we call the Lord Mayor 'Your Worship'; but we don't ever use it for people we meet in our own everyday lives.

When I try to express to myself what I mean by 'worship' and why it is important in my relationship with God, I find myself thinking in different terms. It is not to do with ceremonies and stately pomp but with the way in which I express an attitude. It includes for me practical expressions of love. It is something which I cannot fully understand or put into words, but which I can communicate in my actions and by the way in which I perform those actions. It includes a very fierce sense of loyalty together with the assurance that God has an even stronger loyalty to me. It includes a sense of wonder and awe that I am permitted a close relationship with someone so far above and beyond me in every sense. And underneath everything, it expresses how much I appreciate the spiritual, mental and emotional 'arm round the shoulders' that speaks of companionship, protection, mutual enjoyment and loving care. The Bible expresses it like this: '. . . underneath are the everlasting arms' (Deuteronomy 33:27).

For me, the word 'praise' conjures up the picture of someone jumping up and down, shouting with excitement and glee. It is often related to a specific incident and to something performed or achieved, for which I want to thank God. 'Worship' on the other hand has a greater solemnity, and suggests to my mind the picture of someone down on their knees or on their face, speechless with gratitude and joy because of the person in whose presence they are. It has to do more with God's 'being' than with his 'doing'.

Who is God?
'Worship' is often slower to develop in children than 'conversational prayer' because of the way in which we come to know God. I understood God to be my Father long before I understood what is implied by his titles Creator, Saviour or Judge. I think this is important. If a child learns to know and love a parent within a secure, caring family relationship then he can later put other facets of that parent's character and behaviour into their

proper context.

I remember the very first time I saw my father speaking in the court of law where he worked. He was a receiver, and his job involved presenting to the court cases against company directors or managers whose actions had caused their companies to fail, sometimes for criminal reasons. On this particular day, he was planning to expose the fraudulent practices of one man. His manner and the way he conducted himself made a deep impression on me and opened up a new understanding of why he did and said certain things at home.

I was young at the time – perhaps thirteen or fourteen years old – pigtail dangling down my back, round, blue, plastic-rimmed spectacles constantly slipping down my nose. Staring out through them, I could use my imagination to characterise all the people there in court: silent, stern, sitting in their special places. Who were they all? The ones in robes I knew. They gave me the shivers. There were two barristers. One of them, a little white wig incongruously perched on his curly dark hair, thumbs stuck behind the lapels of his black gown, kept turning to the grey man in a pinstripe suit who sat beside him, holding out his hand for papers and big legal tomes, their pages marked with raggy slips of paper. Everything was very stern and forbidding. The judge, sitting high up on the bench above the court, was an old man with a title and a sagging jowl. He had half-glasses, red robes and a long grey wig.

My father, very tall, very thin, dark hair, dark suit, dark tie, all papers and concentration, walked up into the witness-box. On the direction of the judge, he affirmed that he would 'tell the truth, the whole truth and nothing but the truth' and got on with his case. As he went gravely and clearly through point after point, it seemed to me that he was slowly damning the man whose criminal dabblings in his company's finances were the cause of this sombre occasion.

I was the only visitor in court; this was not an occasion to thrill the public but it was grim and timeless, a ceremonious conducting of the affairs of justice, dispensing with integrity the appropriate response laid down in The Law.

And my father was part of it. I felt that here in court was someone I did not really know at all; and I was particularly glad that I knew him better as my father, rather than as this stern, deep-voiced, forbidding man who stood very still, reading from a sheaf of papers, or squaring his shoulders to look at the judge as he replied quietly and with authority to specific questions. It would have been hard to have met him for the very first time in court, and to have tried subsequently to have a social relationship with him! Here, he was not a 'social' being at all but an impartial and in many ways impersonal embodiment of a solemn and upright system. I remember having a nervous giggle to myself as I considered the reaction of the rest of the court if I had suddenly stood up and said, 'Er . . . Daddy . . .' when *I* had wanted clarification of a point!

Yet I had a relationship with him. That was why I had come. I wanted to see what he was involved in; he wanted me to understand something more of the workings of justice. As I went out through the long, echoing, mosaic–floored chamber that forms the entrance to the Courts of Justice and on into the old streets of London past the place where the Temple Bar once stood, I was still caught up in the solemn, timeless dignity of a system that seemed totally dependable and beyond corruption or even decay.

God is also solemn when he is in his court of law. Yet if we know him as Father, we know for certain that God, who is also our judge, is *not* capricious or sadistic. He does *not* enjoy the pain felt by his creatures when they fall and get hurt. We know that he is concerned for the overall good – ours in particular, but everyone else's as well; and that concern for the integrity of the universe he has created, makes absolute upright justice a vital part of that character so that I am able to have complete confidence in it.

Loyalty to God

Real love leads to loyalty; the deeper the love grows, the more stable the relationship, and the stronger the ties of allegiance and loyalty. This is where one takes the first steps in worship. We cannot worship a God who belongs only to the grimness of the court, to the presentation of a case where every evidence is incontrovertible and towards whom we feel no loyalty, no sense of relationship, only his impartiality without understanding. That would breed fear. We have to come to God with a clear understanding of his relationship to us as our loving Father first, because loyalty which grows from love is one of the most basic ingredients of worship.

Loyalty often grows out of the experience of dependence. This means that we can teach our children the elements of worship from an early age. Most children know that they need their parents, and that even when they feel angry with us, they cannot cope without us. They also know that, when they have got to the end of the extreme emotions, we will still be there, dependable and providing.

One day when Gavin had been punished for something, he went off to think things over by himself. By the time I had found him sitting, elbows-on-knees, chin-in-hand, under a bush in the garden, he had more or less regained his equilibrium, but he informed me seriously, 'Really and truly, I would have preferred to run away from home, and one day, if things go on like this, I'm afraid I really might have to!' Then he added that he was afraid it would be silly to go off without money or food and without having thought about where he was going *to*; because then he would have to turn back soon and ask for help, 'And then I would look stupid, wouldn't I?'

Even in his frustration and anger, even though he accepted that the punishment he had been given was just, even with the sharp desire to run away from the problem and hopefully hurt us all in the process, he was devastatingly aware of who would be hurt most. He knew how futile his attempt was likely to be and that he was, as yet, unable to cope alone, however much he wanted to. We talked about his feelings later, when the original cause had been forgotten.

That's often how we relate to God. He wants us to do the right things, to follow the laws that he has in his wisdom set down as leading to the duties that allow true freedom. He wants us to learn that all wrongs bring consequences hurtful to the wrongdoer and usually to others as well. (Remember the story of Jonah?)

Sometimes when we have gone about things in the wrong way we get frustrated and angry and try to run away from God. We want to forget the upsetting situation and hit back at him. But we know deep down that in the end we need him and we've got to come back. We don't always come back simply because we need help. If we know him well, we sometimes come back finally because deep down we *want* to, because we really do love him after all and cannot do without sharing that love.

We know that we need God, that we can always depend on him to help us when we need it. Our loyalty to him grows from that. It becomes a deep love and eventually we develop a sense of awe that God is willing to do so much for us when he gets so little, *so* little, in return. This is when we begin to shake our heads in wonder at this God who is also our Father; when we can, in complete humility, just become engulfed in gladness that he is who he is.

Learning to worship

As parents, we can learn more about worship by being willing to take time to think about God; to concentrate for a few moments on who God is; on what he is; on why we think about him in the way we do. It may be that when we try to do that, we will realize that we need to take a bit more time later to think it all over once more and to expand our ideas of God. If a few words from the Bible come into our minds, it's worth looking them up. I keep a Bible concordance close at hand to act as a verse finder, then think about the verses more carefully, in their context. If we accept that the Bible really is God speaking his thoughts, then we will most certainly get to know more about God as we share his thoughts. Sometimes I get overwhelmed by thinking about God. Then I tend to rifle through my classical music and play something to help me express to God how I feel about him, asking him to turn this expression of worship into something more than an emotional reaction and to give me some practical opportunity during the day to express that worship. Other people won't be interested in using classical music in that way, but perhaps there is something else you can use in the same way. Think about the ways in which you 'worship' God. How can we develop our ideas and practices, and how can we pass on those ideas to our children? One way could be to discuss the meaning behind a daily Bible reading with them. We can ask them what *they* think it means. We can encourage them to come to God thoughtfully to talk over with him their understanding of who he is. As that understanding grows, so it will affect their daily lives.

Romans 12:1 reminds us that worship is to do with the loving commitment of every aspect of our lives to the God who is so much more than just our Father. As we begin to grasp – and act out – the significance and totality of that commitment, our worship will develop and deepen. As it does so, it will inevitably make us want to help our children expand their understanding of God. This is what worship is all about.

Ideas and activities

Worship is about expressing our love for God through our actions and in our words. The following ideas aim to help children understand more about the meaning of worship and can be used as part of a family worship time.

1 Read a short Psalm of praise aloud together, for example, Psalm 100.
2 Ask the children: Why do we worship God? Encourage them to think about the Psalm you have read for some ideas.
3 Ask the children in what ways some of the following could be good places or ways in which to worship God:

* Sitting in a church congregation
* Relaxing in your favourite comfortable chair at home
* Reading the Bible before you go to bed
* Travelling on a crowded bus or train
* Helping Mum prepare dinner
* Singing as you walk along a beautiful country lane
* Praying with your family
* Making friends with someone in your class who is always on their own.

4 Take a large sheet of paper and write on it: 'God is . . .' Ask everyone to write on the paper their ideas of what they think God is like (eg good, holy, big, love, Father etc). Then ask each person to think about what they have written.

* In what ways does this make God different from us?
* Has God seemed like that in a particular way to you recently? When? How?
* Does it make you want to be more like that?

Stick up the paper as a poster to remind your family of what God is like every time you pray.

Ask everyone to pray a 'thank you prayer' to God for being like the attribute they named, and then add a 'please' to help them to be more like that themselves.

15 Praying for others

Robin gabbled through his prayers. He had some special secret of his own tucked away in his brain, waiting to be brought out and enjoyed once the light was off and it was really, truly bedtime. He remembered to say thank you for an afternoon at the pottery and sorry that he had stamped on Gavin's Lego when he was in a bad mood; he asked for help for Grandpa and Aunty Eunice and Aunty Sandy who were ill; but he was actually thinking about The Secret. He must go through the motions of praying so that he could get rid of Mummy, but really he knew that he was simply repeating empty words for my benefit. He just wanted to get through the process in a hurry, and he didn't actually have any desire to discuss these matters with God.

Many words
Our boys love stories. They have read them aloud, and listen endlessly to favourite stories on cassette tapes. Sometimes they tell themselves stories in their play. We live in a noisy society and from time to time I find myself blotting out the sound of their talk along with everything else. Then a pull at the arm, or a bellow from the front room catches my attention: 'Mummy, are you *listening*?'

I have to confess that I am not, because what they were saying seemed to be just another story told to each other, or perhaps a repeat of what they had already told me – about school or about what terrible things which friend had done to whom when. I had felt they didn't really have need of an audience.

The Bible tells us that we will not be heard for our 'many words' and that we do not need to 'keep on babbling like pagans' (Matthew 6:7). This suggests that God doesn't listen when we repeat things mindlessly.

Some people just talk on because they have never learnt what conversation is all about; or because they are nervous and not relaxed in a situation. Others talk to cover up a lack of action, attempting to substitute words for deeds.

Keep it short!
Because communications are so poor in Lubumbashi, the missionary community has set up a short-wave radio network and it is rare to see a missionary in town without a hand-held transmitter sprouting somewhere from their clothing. When anyone has a message to give, they identify themselves, use the call-sign of the person they wish to contact and wait for a response. When in contact, the message is given and its end is signified by the word 'over'. Messages tend to be short and to the point. Chatting is discouraged. These machines are for business, not pleasure! The radio has to be switched on at all times, and we were grateful to have this contact on the night in 1991 when the shooting started on one side of the town and the orgy of looting and destruction began. Every group was in contact with all the others and we could be sure that we were all aware of what was happening and that everyone was safe. On normal days a radio has a rather different use, perhaps to call me to a medical emergency, or to check with Walter that someone has taken on

the responsibility of collecting from school the eight missionary children from this area of town. It is frustrating when your battery gives up half-way through a transmission, or when some powerful source of interference close at hand blots out a response and you have to use the jargon, 'Sorry – negative copy – please repeat.' It can be equally frustrating (but sometimes amusing as well) when someone's transmit button gets pushed at the wrong moment and everyone suddenly becomes party to the private conversations or home noises going on in someone else's kitchen or living room!

The basic principle of this sort of communication is that you listen constantly and carefully, and respond briefly when you personally are called. Prayer is, of course, more than that; but the idea of listening and responding is fundamental to the concept of prayer.

Learning to intercede

Prayer is not mindless repetition; nor is it simply the business-like response of the radio operator, 'Message received.' There are times when repetition is vital, and when a short, business-like contact with God is simply not enough. In these cases, repetition may have to do with deep concern, a longing for what is right, and a willingness to be personally involved in some serious matter. This type of praying is far from being thoughtless and is not to be entered into lightly. We call it intercession – repeated, pleading prayer with God, in and for a certain situation, and almost always on behalf of someone else. It requires enormous commitment on the part of the one who prays because it involves a sharing in the suffering or experience of the situation being prayed for.

This type of prayer requires some maturity of faith because it is demanding; but it brings with it enormous blessings and a real deepening of one's family experience of God – of that God-given, ideal Father-child relationship. It is in some small way a putting into practice of the sufferings of the Lord Jesus – a far-off sharing – and it has to be voluntary and without coercion. It has a lot to do with looking outwards and being more concerned for others than for self (even the spiritual life of 'self') and with the growing desire to be like Christ in everything. I have to confess that for me this is the most difficult and unexplored area of prayer, even though I know it to be the most fruitful in my own life.

Children can, however, be very deeply involved in intercession. It is quite possible for them to understand the serious nature of a situation and to want to be involved with God in changing that situation. We have had problems with the supply of staff for the day school our children attend here in our city. The school was started by the missionary community but accepts any English-speaking children. It is still relatively new and not well known. With the desperate economic situation and political instability in the country, it is hard to find missionary teachers to fill the vacancies. The suggestion was made that this might mean the partial closure of the school. Gavin, horrified at the prospect of losing some of his school friends, decided to plead earnestly with God to show the school council the best way forward. He told God that what he really wanted was a few more teachers, but that if God had something else in mind, please would he tell us so that we could pray properly so that the school could 'go on being normal'? Every night he prayed a similar prayer, reminding God that this matter was so far unresolved.

Robin has also prayed in the same manner but with less regular commitment for Aunty Eunice. One night when he had heard that her cancer seemed to have spread and that she was very unwell again, he started to pray, 'Please God, please, please *please* make Aunty Eunice better . . .' then he stopped and turned to me. 'Mummy, it might be like Jesus in Gethsemane, mightn't it?' he said thoughtfully. 'He didn't want it to hurt, but he knew what he wanted to get in the end, so he said, "I want to do what you want." '

He closed his eyes and started again. 'Dear Lord Jesus, please let Aunty Eunice know that she's doing what you want, and help her to feel happy in her heart, even if it hurts. For Jesus' sake, Amen.'

Prayers like these in which children (either on their own or with guidance from their parents) learn to stand back from a situation, try to look at it from God's point of view and then make persistent efforts in prayer to bring God's power into a situation to change it, are real intercessory prayers. I have a sneaking suspicion that God might just put more value on such prayers from children than he does on similar prayers from those of us who are more mature and understanding . . .

Praying for our children

As a parent, I feel that physical parenthood brings the opportunity for development in my spiritual life in the realm of intercession. It is easier for most of us to feel deep and longing emotions for our children and their futures than it is to feel so strongly for those vast numbers of unknown or less-known people in the outside world. If we can begin to express to God the desires we have for our own children – for them to come to know him, to grow like him, or whatever seems necessary – then we can begin to gain for ourselves a closeness to God that will have its effect on the way we pray *with* as well as *for* our children, and on the way in which they learn to pray themselves.

Intercession by a parent for a child can and does have lasting effects on that child's life. It is demanding, but I sometimes find myself using my willingness to intercede for the boys as a yardstick to measure my own commitment both to my children and to my God. It acts as a reminder of God's commitment to me, and my need to reciprocate by expressing my commitment to my own sons.

Ideas and activities
Your will be done
1 Help your children to think about how to pray for others by talking about some of the following. Ask them to imagine that each person described is one of their friends. What would they ask God to do for that person?

a) Sarah's father is getting a transfer in his work. That means that either he will have to be away from home all week and at home only at weekends; or that the entire family will have to move to the town where his new job is. Sarah doesn't want to have to leave her home and friends, but she doesn't want her dad to be away from home so much either.

b) Sam's parents have just divorced. Now he has to live some of the time with his mum and some of the time with his dad. He cries a lot because he wants to have his mum and dad and home together like they used to be.

c) Stacey's big brother was in a serious accident and he's been in hospital for a long time. The doctors say he will never walk again. Stacey is angry with God for letting his brother get hurt so badly.

d) The damage from strong winds and floods has forced many people to leave their homes. Claire's parents say that one of the homeless families can stay with them for a few weeks. But Claire does not want to have to share her room or her things with any strangers.

II Ask your children if there is someone they care about who has a big problem at the moment.

* What is the problem?
* What do you want for that person?
* What do you want God to do for that person?
* If Jesus were the one praying for that person, what do you think he would pray for them?

16   Children have problems too!

Gavin's bad day

'I've lost my appetite,' Gavin suddenly announced at supper one night. 'All I really want to do is to go to bed. I've had a *bad day*.'

He had just been told off by his father for shouting at Robin, and that had been the final straw. We let him go off to his room and fetch the inevitable book (his version of a security blanket), to take his mind off the 'bad day' and to let him get his equilibrium back. Children have problems just as much as adults do! Gavin's bad day comprised letting 'at least twenty goals through and I only saved about six' at football during break at school; going to pottery with his friends and finding that not a single one of his precious clay models had been fired, although everyone else in the group had a minimum of two items ready to be taken home; finding that the tyre on his bike was flat and that he really needed a new inner tube – and that size is not to be had in this city at present, so an order would have to be sent abroad for one; and getting roundly told off for something particularly naughty he had been involved in with six other children, but as far as he knew, none of them had got the scolding that he had. It was enough to make you want to crawl off to bed!

Supper (with an unplanned ice cream for dessert), toys in the bath and a story after Bible-reading helped the situation just a little. Bedtime came and as usual I climbed up the side of his bunk-bed as he lay on his front, head propped up on his hands. It was prayer time and tonight Mummy was the one who was going to pray with him. In the bunk below, Robin was snoring peacefully under his mosquito-net. We spread Gavin's net properly, giggling as I got caught in the folds. I switched the light off but it was almost full moon and through the curtains we could feel the deep blueness outside. It gave us enough of a glimmer to see each other, but allowed for a little privacy, too. What did we want to talk to God about tonight?

I suggested to Gavin that he should tell God about The Bad Day.

'What's the point?' he asked indignantly. 'He knows what happened, and he didn't stop all those balls from getting through!'

Nor did I, I pointed out. I knew all about it, too – and I hadn't been able to help at the time, either. Even if I *had* been there, I couldn't have helped. *He* was goalkeeper, not me; but he had wanted to tell me so that he could 'get things off his chest'. Hadn't that helped?

Still indignant, he reminded me that I had laughed when he had told me one of the other disasters of the day. He was right, I had; it had been very funny, and at the time I had given him a hug and told him I thought he was very special.

'Are you cross with me for laughing?' I asked.

'I ought to be,' he replied, 'only afterwards I thought it was funny too so I laughed even though I didn't want to.'

He was aware that there was more than one way of looking at things, and that perspective and distance help; but he was also very much aware of the hurts he felt because of the ways in which, as he saw it, he had

132

failed or others had failed him. Half of his mind was afraid that God might not feel quite so sorry for him as he wanted. The other half had begun to realise that whilst he might be badly injured and in need of attention, he was also only one part of a bigger panorama with greater implications.

Children's problems are just as important as adults' problems. The way in which they learn to deal with them during their early years has an enormous influence on the way in which they cope with problems later in life. Here too as Christian parents, particularly by praying for and with our children, we can have a major impact for good or for mediocrity on their future lives.

Hurt

When I was first making notes for the section of this book dealing with saying thank you to God, the boys had just prayed a very special 'thank you prayer' in the midst of some quite severe problems. Lubumbashi had

133

just seen two nights of devastating looting by an army on the rampage and we and hundreds of other people were sitting camped out in a school, waiting for an escort of foreign soldiers to evacuate us from the country by road. All that we now possessed was in the back of our vehicle. Local friends had brought word that just after the soldiers had accompanied us from our home to the school, our house had been looted by people who smashed what could not be taken away. They had ripped out fitments and wiring and even shot one of the dogs in the knees. Someone had the horrible job of putting her out of her pain. We had to tell the boys that even though we had thought we might be able to return to our house once the initial violence was over, that would no longer be possible. We didn't even have enough things to camp with for long. There would be no school as staff and pupils were all involved in the evacuation too. There would be no toys or books left, and no water or electricity. The city centre was so extensively damaged that we were not sure that people would be able to buy food, and the colour of our skins might make it unsafe for some local folk to be associated with us. For a time anyway, we would have to leave Zaire.

Gavin asked, 'But why do they want our books?' (Most of our books are in English – and we live in a French-speaking country.) Then, 'so what are we going to do now?'

'We'll have to ask God about both those things,' I replied. 'We don't really know at the moment. We have to leave here when we're told. We'll have to ask God what happens after that.'

To this I received the rather scathing reply, 'Of course we have to ask God! But what *else* do we have to do?'

Robin, the practical one, isn't satisfied with spiritualising. Looking up at some of the protecting group of foreign soldiers around the grounds, he said, 'Before we do anything, hadn't we better ask the military first?'

We talked about the need to listen to God and discuss things with him first, and then to be ready to put into practice whatever he said. We explained that it was no good simply to keep repeating the questions 'Why?' and 'What next?' without listening out for an answer and applying it.

The special 'thank you prayer' I spoke of earlier came on the second evening in the tent where we were sleeping. The boys were finding it hard to think of anything to thank God for, as they realised more and more clearly what they had lost. Finally Gavin said, 'I have something I really do want to say thank you for.' He closed his eyes. 'I wish we hadn't lost all our stuff, God,' he said, 'but thank you that we can have a real live adventure – and sleep in a tent as well.'

As adults we know that it is definitely NOT easy to look for the good side of things when we are overwhelmed by our problems; but hurts can be tackled head-on when we try first of all to distance ourselves a little from them and then to look for something genuinely positive around them.

Hurts can also dissolve as the children begin to appreciate how much God cares for and about them individually. Sometimes the boys ask us to tell them stories of things that have happened to us in the past. Their father has some thrilling stories of the way in which God provided for him and the group of missionaries from a station that was deserted by local people as it became a battleground between government and rebel forces; of how God led them out in safety, and how time and time again came the little, loving miracle to assure them that God was with them, caring for them every step of the way. He tells the astonishing story of the escape of their group of missionaries, including an old lady in a wheelchair and a mother well over eight months pregnant. They had to travel by tractor, trailer, moped, pick-up truck and so on through the heat of the day under a sweltering tropical sun. But God knew beforehand when he wanted them to leave. The sky clouded over and for hours they travelled in the cool. On their arrival at a safe stopping-point they realised that they had been travelling through the entire period of a partial eclipse. God cares – so he times things right for his children. (The story of that escape is told in a paperback *Trapped* by David Dawson, published by Regal Books, Gospel Light Publications, California.)

The boys are equally fascinated by my more mundane missionary stories. There was the piece of embroidery to be completed by a group of students, and there was not enough of one colour of silk thread. The very day we were due to meet to finish the work, a parcel arrived from UK posted almost a year before – and in the centre of it was a crushed paper bag containing a few skeins of embroidery thread – all of them the exact same dye-lot as the thread we were needing. Then there was the time when I wanted to purchase a motorbike that was being rebuilt, and didn't have sufficient funds. But the work took longer than expected so the sale date was put off. Meanwhile, I received an unexpected gift of money 'towards transport' that covered not only the cost of the motorbike, but also the insurance, registration and all the paperwork and even left a tiny amount over to show that God gives a 'good measure, pressed down, shaken together and running over' (Luke 6:38).

The boys wanted to know whether God would do that for them too, and after they lost their belongings in the looting, they had plenty of time and opportunities to see that God IS interested in their problems, that he DOES care about them and that he has better ways than they could ever think of to heal their hurts and build them up again. We trust that, as they have seen their parents finding God to be trustworthy and enormously generous, they too will come to understand that God really does have answers to their hurts – if they will only come and ask him for healing.

Death
Children often understand more than we give them credit for concerning suffering and death. Whilst they cannot usually see the wide range of implications of a death, they can accept the facts and share some of the feelings adults experience following a bereavement. In fact, I have found that a child's uncluttered thinking can be a real help to me in my own attempts to deal with the same thing.

When we were on leave a few years ago, a long-time friend of my family's (I'll call him Mr Brown) was suffering from terminal cancer. The site of the growth led to some severe pain and considerable suffering. It was suffering shared by his family as they watched him dying. Our family was unable to visit, but kept in touch and prayed regularly for the necessary strength and comfort for all of them. One day we received the news that Mr Brown had died.

Bedtime prayer time came round, and Gavin, aware of our sadness and mixed emotions, announced that he had a special 'thank-you prayer' about Mr Brown that he wanted to say to God.

'Father God,' he began, 'thank you that Mr Brown died today. Did you just call down to him and say, "Well, Mr Brown, I think this has gone on just *too long* now, don't you? I really think you've had enough, and I don't think you want any more hurting, do you. Wouldn't you like to come home now and have a rest? There's a lot of room up here and Mrs Brown can come up as well later on." Is that what you said? And I think Mr Brown said, "Yes, please – I would like to really – as long as you can explain to Mrs Brown." Then you said, "All right then – come on." And now he's well again and you're looking after him, God, and that's good. But can you please tell Mrs Brown that he really *needed* a break – and so did she – and that you'll tell her when she can come up and see him? I expect she'll be rather lonely otherwise.'

He opened his eyes. 'Mummy, can we go and see Mrs Brown sometime? I want to give her a hug for him. Do you think that would help?'

You can probably imagine that I was in tears myself by this time as I realised how God was using a young child's clear, simple faith to teach me not only how I ought to be reacting to the apparently premature death of a friend, but also how I should be viewing the needs of his family. And it was Gavin's relationship with God, expressed in his praying, that brought the ability to understand and react positively to a situation largely beyond his grasp. Learning that God is in charge and bringing good out of the most impossible of all problems to solve *must* give a child a firm, solid foundation on which to stand when he faces other problems in his daily life.

Peer pressure
One of the most difficult problems for both parents and children to deal with is the pressure to conform exerted by other children in their own peer group. However keen a child might be to do what appears to be right, it is extremely difficult for a child to consider standing out from the crowd and being different – and alone. Childhood is where we learn to live in a group, where we learn how to deal with other people, and where we learn how much human beings need each other.

Group pressures should not be underestimated and we do our children a great disservice if we *demand* that they stand out and be different. Children deserve enormous praise if they manage to see the rights and wrongs of a situation and DO stand up for the right; but they should never be made to feel that we have been badly let down by them if they cannot. To stand out in a crowd of peers demands a sharp, sophisticated awareness of the situation, and an ability to assess it, together with the ability to determine a right response and to carry it out. Many, many times I have as an adult failed to do the right thing in a difficult situation and it is unfair to expect my children, with much less experience, to do better than me. God understands our feelings. If he is prepared to accept how hard it is for us, then as parents we can't be harder than that on our children.

A child can be helped with the problem of adverse peer pressure if he can be made aware of the job of his conscience, is able to listen for that conscience, and has been instructed in what is right and what is wrong. He needs to be sure that God can help him in such problem times and situations. From my own childhood I can remember occasions when I was too scared to say or do anything that would have made me 'stand out'. I also remember occasions when I was able to shout a 'help' to God and then saw the situation changing in front of my eyes so that the problem simply dissolved or changed – without my having to do or say anything.

Once at junior school I had been given a message to pass on to my class teacher, asking her to take school assembly as the headmistress was occupied with a parent. When I got back to my classroom with the message, the teacher was not there. I had been given other errands as well, so I left the message with a group of classmates and carried on. I finished delivering attendance registers just as the bell sounded for assembly and slipped into my place in the school hall as the rest of the classes came filing in. Nobody came to take assembly. There was a long wait, in almost total silence. I tried to whisper to find out if the message had been passed on. Nobody would reply. I dared not whisper again, or I would draw attention to myself.

Then in through the double doors came the class teacher and glared at us. She was quite angry. 'Who failed to pass on the message to me?' she demanded. I waited for the children concerned to own up. Nobody said a word. I was just beginning to panic as one of the girls pointed her finger at me. I remember praying desperately. 'What now, God?' because I didn't dare 'tell' but I wasn't going to accept the blame I felt I didn't deserve! At that precise moment a boy came into the hall and spoke to the teacher.

'The headmistress wants me,' my teacher said. 'Mrs Brown, could you carry on with Prayers, please?'

I never heard anything more about the incident – and I was still regularly given errands to do. It must have been sorted out somewhere . . . God knows. He understands. He acts.

One practical way in which parents can help their children to withstand negative peer pressure, for example at school, is to encourage contacts between Christian staff and children, and between a Christian in an older class and a younger child. The friendship and support of age and authority lend a good deal of weight to the arguments of a younger child who is battling to say and do what is right. 'I think I'll just go and find Jane' can be not only a let-out when someone does not want to be involved in dubious pranks or wrongdoings; it can also make others think twice too, without leaving the impression of tale-telling or whining.

Wishes

All children wish that certain things could happen to or for them. Many such 'wishes' are impossible, but there is often an underlying desire that we adults can discover and maybe help to fulfil. Some things which are real problems to children seem trivial to us; but God can take those problems, if they are brought to him, and do something special with them.

When Gavin was almost five years old we travelled to my husband's home town in New Zealand. The dog-leg trip took us from Africa to England, on to Japan and finally to the other side of the world, to New Zealand. We had looked at many maps and globes to show Gavin where we were going, which countries we would expect to fly over and what sort of things he could expect to see. Unlike most five year olds, Gavin had been privileged to go right round the world twice already, by different routes each time, and has as a result developed early a good sense of geography. For a long time he had been wanting to visit the 'frozen North' and in particular Alaska. Unfortunately it is not the most common route to go to New Zealand via the Arctic, and as the date of our return came near Gavin asked for the umpteenth time, 'Mummy, will I ever be able to go there?'

'I expect so,' I replied, 'one day when you are grown up you might try and go there for a holiday.'

This, of course, was a totally unsatisfactory answer. From then on at every bedtime he pleaded earnestly with God that he would be able to visit Alaska one day.

During our return journey we had one of those interminable airport waits between flights. We snoozed, took the boys for walks, read all the sign-boards, snorted at the prices of things in airports, read stories, drew and did all the other things one thinks up to do to try and entertain children in such situations. Our flight was, of course, delayed. When we were just about at the end of our tether, Walter took Gavin for a final look at the flight board to see whether there was any news of our flight. And there was the notice: our flight number for London *via Alaska*, with a refuelling stop at Anchorage! We could hardly believe our eyes. We had not come by that route and had been told that we would return the same way that we had come out.

We spent an hour or more out of the plane at Anchorage and so were able to go up to the roof viewing area to get a look at the hills and valleys of Alaska in the spring.

During the rest of the flight Gavin was able to see the Northern Lights and to watch an enormous iceberg break up and send a huge plume of spray high into the air as we passed overhead. As he settled down to sleep in his seat, his 'thank you prayer' went something along these lines: 'Dear Lord Jesus, it was nice of you to let me come to Alaska so soon after I asked you to. It was really good. I hadn't expected it, you know, so it was a surprise. I like surprises. But I still want to come back again and see it in the snow some time. You won't forget please, will you? Amen.'

Help for hurts

Some of the problems children experience may seem, to adult eyes, very minor. Sadly, however, life's major problems – division, separation, death, loss, violation, frustration and a multitude of other hurts don't pass children by untouched. These have to be faced and dealt with if they are not to become themselves the cause of more problems in the future.

Maybe these problems do not all have answers. There are places in God's book where people never find out the 'reason why'. Job didn't. Jeremiah was taken forcibly to the place where God had – through him – strictly forbidden the fleeing Jews to go. Joseph had years of hardship before his problems were sorted out. Sometimes, though, answers do come promptly (eg Elijah and the widow), but not always.

We have seen God helping our own children face up to and work through some of the fairly major problems they have experienced. Usually there is an underlying biblical principle that can be applied to a specific situation, found in stories like those of Job, Joseph or

Elijah. Whatever the problems of the children in our care, what we need, both for ourselves and for them, is an openness to God, so that we can see the appropriate principle and apply it to their particular needs.

Ideas and activities

I Several stories in this chapter contain examples of how we can pray when things go wrong. Look back for some which may fit a situation your family knows about or is presently having to deal with. Share them with your children either by reading them aloud or retelling them. Are there some ideas here which could help you deal with your situation?

II *A family prayer diary.* Set out the pages of a notebook as shown below. Record your prayer requests for yourselves and for others. Write the date when you first begin praying that prayer. Then watch for the answers God gives. Write them down alongside the prayer with the date you receive the answer.

Are the answers always what you expected or wanted? Or does God sometimes like to give surprises in the way he works things out?

PRAYER DIARY			
Date	Prayer	Answer	Date

17   Getting the answers

'Can't you just wait a moment, Robin?'

'But if I wait like usual, I shall be old before you tell me . . .' Poor child! He knew that his mother was too busy to be bothered with him at that moment. Is God ever like that?

When we question whether God really answers our prayers, the most common reply seems to be that God *always* answers us; often it is added that those answers can either be 'yes', 'no', or 'wait'.

For children this is a most unsatisfactory reply. The writer C S Lewis in his book *A Grief Observed* describes the process he went through of feeling shut out from God's presence following the death of his wife. He felt that he was hammering at the gates of heaven only to find that, at his moment of greatest need, there was no one at home. A little later he realised that the question he was asking God did not have an answer. Until he could rephrase his question, there was no answer that God could give. If such a man, who spent much time thinking about his faith, could have such problems, perhaps it is not being honest either with ourselves or our children if we feed them clichés about what they can expect from God by way of answers to their prayers.

Recognising God's answers

Our difficulty in recognising answers – or in accepting them when they are different from the response we expected – may come in part from the predominance of personal concerns in our prayers. A lot of the time, in my experience, our prayers are about ourselves and our own welfare, or that of our immediate family and circle of contacts. The main aim of our lives as Christians should not be to get from God what we feel we have been promised (like the Prodigal Son in the parable in Luke 15), but it should be to grow more like the Lord Jesus Christ.

We can only do this by constantly looking at him, learning about him, talking to him, and consequently finding our love growing – and that we want to please him, work with him and be more and more like him. The effect this has on our lives is that we find ourselves getting concerned, as he was, much more with others and much less with ourselves. This of course is the ideal. Most of us fail to reach it! But the more upward and outward looking we are, the more we will be able to say at the end of our prayers, 'Please Father, will you do this, because the Lord Jesus wants it quite as much as I do?'

If we can honestly say that at the end of a special time of prayer, then of course we can be sure that God will do what we ask. I have found that it is easier to be sure that he wants something when we are praying it for someone else, than it is when we are asking for something for ourselves!

It is necessary to examine our own lives from time to time, but this century has seen a movement back to the inward-holiness ideas that led the church in earlier centuries away from missionary zeal and into the development of hermitages and the cloistered life. While this may be the calling for some, we need to remember that Jesus' disciples were commissioned to be *apostles*

– those sent out to others. They were told by the Lord Jesus himself to go *out* and spread the good news. They were not told to keep it to themselves, hoping that simply by their example people would come to know God. By spending too much time looking inside ourselves I fear that we can sometimes use the condition of our own spiritual lives as an excuse for not spending as much time as we should in passing on the good news about Jesus.

I have many times heard people expressing the view, 'I must get my own walk with the Master right before he can use me for his work.' In that case, we must all become perfect before God can use us! That is not a doctrine I find in my Bible. We must, of course, be walking *with* him before he can use us, and before we can hear him clearly, but that walk has to be a *forward* one with him beside us, not one with eyes down, perpetually dissecting my own spiritual condition and so failing to look up at the way ahead. It must also be a walk with my face towards God, walking towards him – which is the only position in which my face will ever be able to reflect his likeness.

It is significant that the disciples required time together as a group of Jesus' followers to be able to appreciate this for themselves. Even after the resurrection and the ascension of the Lord Jesus they still had to wait for the coming of the Holy Spirit before they could rid themselves of that inward-looking, closed-in feeling and go out and work effectively for the Lord Jesus.

Things are not often quite so dramatic these days. We don't expect tongues of fire, rushing winds and foreign languages to accompany every realisation of the commission of the Lord Jesus to every individual amongst his followers. We don't read that these things happened, for example, to Paul and Barnabas as they set out on their first missionary journey (Acts 13), nor to the Ethiopian chancellor of the exchequer on his way back to Queen Candace (Acts 8). These manifestations were vital signs in the early church to prove to the world that this was no ordinary, man-made sect. Even now in certain circumstances God does use extraordinary happenings when he wants to demonstrate his power in a special way; but if we wait for such a demonstration before being willing to serve God, we are not going to progress very far in our Christian lives. In order for us to recognise God's answers to our prayers, we should not need to receive spectacular calls from the skies, but should be able to rely on daily, regular conversation with him. I am more likely to recognise my husband's voice than I am to recognise the voice of someone on the radio thundering a message over the air-waves, because I know my husband better and am constantly hearing his voice.

Sometimes we seem to think that God's answers must of necessity be startling, eye-catching and awakening. They aren't! They can be as mundane as the answer we give to the children's 'Please may I have a drink now?' or as exciting as the answers to such questions as, 'Look quick . . . have I passed my exam?' I am convinced that God as my Father feels much the same way about his children as I do about mine; and happily replies to my questions in the same way I might to the children: 'Yes, help yourself; take whatever drink you want,' or 'Hooray, hooray! You got 100%! Come and be hugged!' In both of those cases, the child is waiting for the answer before proceeding. We also need to expect God to answer, but to be willing not to put the reply into his mouth for him!

The more *outward* looking we are, and the more concerned we are for others, the more we will know what to pray for. As we grow up we don't need to ask for a drink; we can just go and get it for ourselves. Soon we will be asking whether we can get a drink for anyone else at the same time. The first time we want to offer a drink to a thirsty stranger we might need to ask whether we may. As we grow we also begin slowly to discern the differences between those who are in real need of water to quench their thirst and those who are looking for something else, for whom the initial expression of thirst is merely a 'lead-in'. And as we grow, we find increasingly that we do not need permission to act on that God-given understanding.

Trust and obey

Sometimes we get 'hung up' on the problem of answers to prayers, because we are not looking at things from the right angle. We know what we want, and are looking for that thing. We may not be open enough to realise that God has sent us an answer, but it is of a different nature from the one we were expecting. So what is the 'correct angle'? It is here that trust, obedience and an open mind come in.

Answers are God's side of the conversation when it is we who have done the asking. Equally, they are our side of the conversation when it is God who has done the asking. When we are waiting for an answer from God, it can sometimes be helpful to look back on our 'conversation' with him. Was it really two-way? Or were we just presenting God with a list of wants? Talking to God, listening to him, worshipping him and learning to be like him mean that we can differentiate (usually!) between the 'yes', 'no' and the 'wait' answers, the questions he asks in return, and the answers that are simply replies in an ongoing conversation between two people who are close to one another.

As the boys grow up I want to be able to recognise and point out to them answers to questions we have put to God as a family. This requires that I should be able to recognise those answers when they come, and that I should be willing to apply them in my own life or in the life of my family. Doing this has given me opportunities on occasion to make leaps in my own Christian life that I might never have considered had it not been for the stimulus provided by the children.

We need to feel assured that God knows what we are really asking. He knows the real need behind the question and he treats us in the appropriate way. Our needs are emotional and mental as well as physical and spiritual and he knows that better than we do. He does not necessarily confine himself to an exact supply of our demand, but treats us with loving concern, as we try to do with our own children.

It was delightful for us to see the boys beginning to understand God's personal love for them as he answered their specific requests after the looting. They are still young in years and in faith and are still largely asking God for things for themselves and for people in their immediate circle, and God answers them accordingly. After the looting, the loss of a knitted toy and the bike were great causes of sadness. Slowly the boys have seen that God can not only replace, but also take away the sadness that was associated with the initial loss. One night when we were in England after the looting, I suggested that Robin should say thank you for the many good things he and Gavin had received since their arrival there, especially since they had been given things they had always wanted when abroad but had never had.

He decided that this was a good sort of prayer and his conversation with his Father went along these lines, 'Dear God, do you know that we never actually *asked* for all these things? I don't know why you gave them to us, then! We didn't ask for them but we got them anyway! Thank you Lord Jesus for all the books and things. I'm glad you just knew that we wanted them. It was very nice of you to send them even when we didn't have birthdays – and there's so *much*! Amen.'

As the children learn that God provides abundantly what we *don't* need as well as those things we do, we trust that they will learn that he is an extravagant God when it comes to giving. After all, if he could give himself to and for us, then we don't need to worry that he will fail to give, joyfully and generously, whatever he sees that it is good for us to have.

A recent incident confirmed to us how important reinforcement of an idea can be to the children's growth in faith and understanding.

When Grandpa's treatment for cancer left him with a deaf ear and an almost-blind eye and without functioning salivary glands, the boys prayed long and fervently for healing for him. One night when Grandpa was here in Zaire, packing up his things and getting ready to retire to England, Robin got the giggles during prayers. 'Dear Lord Jesus,' he prayed, 'please heal Grandpa's blind eye so that he will be able to see again, and his deaf ear so he can hear again; and help him to get back his saliva so that' (snort) 'he can spit again.' Grandpa had a few words to say to Robin about that

one! But some time later we received a letter written from England in which Grandpa said, 'Robin will be glad to know that my remaining salivary gland has stepped up output so I don't need to swill everything down with so much drink. A big thank-you to Robin for his prayers . . .'

When we read it to Robin, after the initial hilarity he gave a thoughtful 'hmm', put his chin in his hands and said, 'I suppose that means that it's worth keeping on reminding God about something, doesn't it?'

That's a lesson about prayer and God's answers that's worth learning, even when you are only six years old!

Ideas and activities
I If you have decided to start a family prayer diary (see page 143), look back at it from time to time with your children to see what answers God has given you.

* Does God seem to be ignoring some of your requests or questions?
* Is it possible that you need to change what you asked God?
* Are you honestly able to make each of those requests 'in Jesus' name' (ie 'I believe this is what Jesus wants too')?

II *Share a story.* Parents, think back to times when God has answered your own prayers or the prayers of someone you know. Share these experiences with your children. Encourage them to share their own stories of answered prayers.

18 Prayer works

Prayer works. That is perhaps one of the most important things we can ever teach our children. Prayer is
contact with God, bringing us into touch with him day
by day, moment by moment as we learn to communicate
with him and allow him to communicate with us.

A growing relationship
Prayer is not a special hot-line set aside for emergency
use. Neither is it a cable connection to a catalogue
shopping company! We cannot simply use prayer as a
citizen's demand for the emergency services, nor as
though we were ordering something that we have
chosen to possess (and have to pay for).

Prayer *is* the type of conversation that denotes a
loving relationship between a growing child and a
caring, wise, generous parent. I notice with our two
boys that the more they think about what their father
does, the more they tend to adopt his mannerisms, walk
like him, use his phraseology in speech and try to do
things in the way he does. And the more they hate it
when misguided adults say to them, 'Whatever would
your father say if he could see you doing that?'

We have thought about a number of different aspects
of prayer. It is the primary contact we have with God,
made not because I want God to know about me but

because I want to know about him. It is a communication system that develops as I use it more and get to know him better; and it matures and changes as I mature and change in my spiritual life. Prayer is also an expression of the Father-child relationship between God and his children, and so demands that I act like a member of the family if I am expecting him to act towards me like a Father.

There are many types of prayer, just as we hold many types of conversation in a family. All are valid, and all play a different role in the growing relationship; and all are necessary to the growth of that relationship. Prayer requires that we listen as well as speak, and that we obey as well as request. It requires practice and commitment, which will develop naturally if the relationship between us and God is a stable, loving one.

Prayer as communication with God has a flip-side where we get the opportunity to think in detail about what *God* wants to communicate to *us*. This is our reading and understanding the Bible, which we sometimes call 'God's word'. This gives us a chance to think over the implications of the relationship and allows us to discuss God's feelings about different issues as well as our own. Together prayer and Bible reading show us the God who wants us to be his children; and they show how important it is that we are honest with God and with ourselves.

We looked at ways in which we could pray – when, how and what – most of which will be determined by our own individual situations; and at ways in which we as parents can mature in our own prayer lives by praying with others and getting to grips with larger needs and concerns than those of our own immediate family and local friends. This often leads into a deeper, more complex and satisfying relationship with God through worship and intercession. It enables us to meet problems squarely, expecting an answer from God but refusing to put that answer into his mouth for him. It teaches us to open our eyes and ears and to be more observant, more willing to thank than to complain, more willing to try what God sets before us and less willing to push it away, saying that we don't like it, before we have even tried it.

Prayer, when it really *is* a two-way conversation, helps us to grow and develop normally. It teaches us wisdom by using God's experience rather than our own, and so keeps us from going through a lot of bad times ourselves before we learn the hard way (at least, it works like that sometimes – if we let it!). Prayer helps us to understand why we react in the way we do and, more importantly, why other people react in the way they do. It helps us to be more understanding, a little more forbearing, more caring or more helpful. In a word, it helps us to become more like the Lord Jesus.

It is not easy, and at times can be a real uphill struggle. There are plenty of times when we stop praying altogether, just as there are times when our children seem to stop growing. Then the children tend to put on a spurt and people who haven't seen them for some time comment, 'My! You've grown all of a sudden!' That can sometimes happen in our Christian lives too.

Listen and obey
There is, however, a big difference between spiritual and physical growth. Spiritual growth depends largely on the daily practice of one word – obedience. If God speaks to us and we hear what he is saying and either ignore it or refuse to put into practice what he is telling us, we will almost certainly fall flat on our faces. It is not the end of the world. God knows what we are like, and most of us tend to be the same in this respect. However, as we grow in other areas, God will begin to demand some obedience from us if he is to continue to give us the answers or help we require.

Before we were married, Walter and I were both struck by some comments in Elisabeth Elliot's book *A Slow and Certain Light*. One chapter suggested that, when you don't know what to do next in any given situation, you should just go ahead and do the next thing. It might sound silly, but it is very practical. When a toddler has once learnt to walk, it stops looking at its feet at every step it takes. When it is going somewhere, it just goes, without too much thought about how. If we are walking in the direction of God's leading in our Christian lives, we need to keep looking to the goal ahead, and not constantly watching our feet.

After the looting of Lubumbashi we went back to England for a time to be close to Walter's father who was having treatment for cancer. Once we heard that he had got a provisional 'all clear' we felt able to consider returning to Zaire. But should we? We had heard that very few expatriates had returned. Most of the business community who had gone back had simply gone to sell up what they had left and quit. A handful of missionaries was there but communication was difficult and the situation unsettled and we could not in all fairness ask any of them to make a decision for us. Was it safe to take the boys back? Where would we stay? Would there be any work for us to do? What about schooling for the children? Walter wanted to go back at the end of January, when we had been in the UK two months. I wanted the children to have some stability and to spend at least the larger part of a school term in one place. I had no real peace of mind about going back to Zaire, but then I had none about staying in England either! Was I getting too attached to the easier life in England? (I might have been if it hadn't been so cold!!)

Some experienced, older Christians from a local church lovingly gave up time to come and pray with us over the situation, and in the end we brought the question down to the basics. We knew that God had originally sent us to Central Africa. There were therefore three questions to answer now, and they depended on each other. First, had God rescinded that call? If the answer was no, then a second question was posed. Was God telling us to be willing to divide the family, so that Walter could go back but the boys and I should stay in England? If the answer to that one was no, then a third question arose. We had had several requests to go and help other mission-stations in neighbouring Zambia, to do jobs we were qualified to do. Should we be considering them instead?

In the end we concluded that his call to us was still valid; so we must return to Central Africa. We had to vacate the missionary home where we were staying by the end of March, and through a 'fluke' (that is, not through our request, but was it God's timing?), we had return tickets to Zambia dated the end of March. We did not feel that dividing the family was right, particularly at that time when there had been lots of changes and adjustments to make already. The boys did not need yet more. We simply had to get up and go, and take things from there. The third question had to wait.

For me that proved to be one of the hardest steps of obedience in my life up to that time. I wanted to go back, but I did not want to expose the boys to potential danger. I wanted to get back to work, but I wanted it to be the work I was previously involved in, not something different. I wanted to 'go home', but we had no home to go to. I wanted a voice from heaven or even a deep peace in my heart to convince me that I was doing the right thing. I didn't get them. I had to tell God that I wanted to be obedient to his will (or, at least, that part of me did – the other part I couldn't quite speak for . . .), and then accept that this meant returning to Zambia (the normal route to Lubumbashi) without having made a final decision.

We did it. And once I had become willing to make

that decision, everything began to fall into place. People began to give us quantities of things that would help us to set up home again – to tell us where we could get this, that or the other at a 'good price', to offer us skills and expertise that we lacked. Once we got to Zambia, there was no question any longer. We were going back in. I expect the people who had already returned thought me a bit odd for taking so long to make up my mind, but some people are slower than others to learn! And once we had begun the journey, the certainty of God's will and the peace of mind were there after all.

One of the books the children borrowed from a local library in England told the story of a space commander who has been disabled while trying heroically to save his ship from disaster. In the story, the commander instructs the first officer what to do to save the space mission. The first officer has a little experience in the matter under discussion, listens, but thinks he knows better and does something else. The captain has to exert superhuman effort to set things right again. Much the same thing recurs throughout the story until, in the end, the only way to save the mission and the lives of the crew is to lock up the first officer who beats on his prison doors in rage and frustration unable to learn his lesson and still thinking that he knows best.

The moral is clear: disobedience can bring disaster, not only on yourself but on many others with whom you are in contact; and the long-term effect is bondage and frustration.

If we as parents are not listening to God and obeying him, how can we possibly teach our children to listen and obey? We remain then, spiritual children still, looking at our own selfish interests without being able to see that they are self-destructive. How can children safely bring up children? If we are concerned to teach our children how to get to know their God, we must teach them how to pray. And we cannot do that unless we have at least begun to learn it for ourselves.

Ideas and activities
I *Prayer is . . .*
Which of these would you say best describes prayer?

* A special hot-line for emergency use
* A cable connection to a catalogue shopping company
* A loving relationship between a growing child and a caring, wise, generous parent
* Contact with God not because I want him to know more about me but because I want to know about him
* A communication system between me and God that develops as I use it more and get to know him better.

II If you have decided to start a family prayer diary (see page 143), remember to look back in a few weeks' time at what you and your children have been asking God.

* Are most of those prayers like the first two in the list above?
* Do they show that you and God have a growing friendship?
* Do you know God better now than when you first started your diary?
* Do any of your questions ask God something about himself?

Ask God to help you all to listen more carefully so that you will increasingly be able to hear and recognise God's voice when he speaks to you.

Bibliography

I Can Talk to God, Helen Caswell, Lutterworth, 1989.

You Can Change the World, Jill Johnson, Operation Mobilisation, 1993.

A Bunch of Green Bananas, David Gatward, Kevin Mayhew, 1993.

Teaching Children to Pray, Keith Wooden, Zondervan, USA, 1993.

And All the Children Said 'Amen', Ian Knox, Scripture Union, 1994.

King Street, reading series for pre-school children, Scripture Union.

Find Out, Bible reading series for parents to use with 5s–7s, Scripture Union.

Quest – help with daily Bible reading for 7s–11s, Scripture Union.

One to One – help with daily Bible reading for 10s–13s, Scripture Union.

Teaching Toddlers the Bible, V. Gilbert Beers, Victor Books (USA).

Become like a Child, Kathryn Copsey, Scripture Union, 1994.

Will my Rabbit go to Heaven? Jeremie Hughes, Lion Publishing, 1988.

All about God, Mary Rose Pearson, Tyndale House, USA, 1993.

1001 Ways to Introduce your Child to God, Kathy Reimer, Tyndale House, USA, 1992.

The A–Z of Ministry with Children, Owen Shelley, Scripture Union Australia, 1992.

101 Questions Children ask about God, Veerman, Galvin, Wilhon, Lucas and Osborne, Tyndale House, USA, 1992.